Better Homes and Gardens®

STEP-BY-STEP

Cabinets
& Shelves

Better Homes and Gardens® Books
Des Moines, Iowa

Better Homes and Gardens® Books
An imprint of Meredith® Books

Step-by-Step Cabinets and Shelves
Editor: Paula Marshall
Art Director: Lynda Haupert
Copy Chief: Catherine Hamrick
Copy and Production Editor: Terri Fredrickson
Contributing Copy Editor: Steve Hallam
Technical Editor: Ed Malles
Contributing Proofreaders: Dan Degen, Kenya McCullum, Margaret Smith
Electronic Production Coordinator: Paula Forest
Editorial and Design Assistants: Kaye Chabot, Mary Lee Gavin, Karen Schirm
Production Director: Douglas M. Johnston
Book Production Managers: Pam Kvitne, Marjorie J. Schenkelberg

Produced by Greenleaf Publishing, Inc.
Publishing Director: Dave Toht
Writer: Steve Cory
Art Director: Jean DeVaty
Design: Melanie Lawson Design
Associate Designer: Rebecca JonMichaels
Illustrators: Jonathan Clark, Dick Ticcioni
Additional Photography: Dan Stultz

Cover Photograph: Scott Little
Cover Design and Production: David Jordan

Meredith® Books
Editor in Chief: James D. Blume
Design Director: Matt Strelecki
Managing Editor: Gregory H. Kayko
Executive Shelter Editor: Denise L. Caringer

Director, Sales & Marketing, Retail: Michael A. Peterson
Director, Sales & Marketing, Special Markets: Rita McMullen
Director, Sales & Marketing, Home & Garden Center Channel: Ray Wolf
Director, Operations: George A. Susral

Vice President, General Manager: Jamie L. Martin

Better Homes and Gardens® Magazine
Editor in Chief: Jean LemMon
Executive Building Editor: Joan McCloskey

Meredith Publishing Group
President, Publishing Group: Christopher M. Little
Vice President, Consumer Marketing & Development: Hal Oringer

Meredith Corporation
Chairman and Chief Executive Officer: William T. Kerr

Chairman of the Executive Committee: E. T. Meredith III

All of us at Better Homes and Gardens® Books are dedicated to providing you with information and ideas to enhance your home. We welcome your comments and suggestions. Write to us at: Better Homes and Gardens® Books, Shelter Editorial Department, 1716 Locust St., Des Moines, IA 50309-3023.

If you would like to purchase any of our books, check wherever quality books are sold. Visit our website at bhgbooks.com or bhg.com.

Note to the Reader: Due to differing conditions, tools, and individual skills, Meredith Corporation assumes no responsibility for any damages, injuries suffered, or losses incurred as a result of following the information published in this book. Before beginning any project, review the instructions carefully, and if any doubts or questions remain, consult local experts or authorities. Because local codes and regulations vary greatly, you always should check with local authorities to ensure that your project complies with all applicable local codes and regulations. Always read and observe all of the safety precautions provided by any tool or equipment manufacturer, and follow all accepted safety procedures.

TABLE OF CONTENTS

INTRODUCTION

Cabinet and shelf projects are, for the most part, affordable, and often can be built without disrupting your home. Set up a work area in your basement, garage, or spare room—someplace that doesn't need to be cleaned up regularly—and you'll have the luxury of being able to leave the project for a few days, returning to it as time allows. Having a separate workroom helps keep a project relaxing and enjoyable.

Step-by-Step Cabinets and Shelves tells you all you need to know to design and build your own shelves or cabinets, and provides plans for specific projects. It will teach you to make shelves that seem to float on the wall, adjustable shelves, stately shelves surrounded by classic moldings, or even simple shelves made by stacking found objects.

The section on kitchen cabinets tells you how to order and install factory-made cabinets, as well as how to build your own. You'll also learn to add custom elements to existing cabinets to make them more attractive and more functional.

The Scope of the Book

Building a set of shelves is many people's first experience with carpentry. It seems as though it ought to be simple—just attach a board to a wall.

But once you get started, you quickly find that even the most simple shelf project can present difficult problems. You'll face these questions:

■ Will the boards be strong enough, and will they last?

■ How do you attach the shelf sturdily without making it look clunky?

■ Is your cabinet or shelf unit really straight, and are the boards level? How can you cut the board ends square and without splinters?

■ What if you want to change the height of different shelves later?

■ How can you give the project a durable and attractive finish?

The fact is, shelf building involves many techniques that are basic to carpentry. To build shelves that look good and last a long time, you need to learn these fundamental methods.

That's why this book includes instructions for measuring, marking, cutting, nailing, and fastening with screws. You don't have to spend lots of money for professional-quality tools, and you don't have to spend weeks learning arcane carpentry skills. But whether you're a rank beginner or a do-it-yourselfer with a few projects under your belt, it is worthwhile to review these techniques and to spend some time practicing them on scrap pieces of wood until you're comfortable with them.

In addition to the fundamentals, cabinetry and shelf building call for special procedures, including: making rabbet, dado, biscuit, and dowel joints; installing hinges and catches; assembling self-contained units; and installing shelf and cabinet hardware. This book teaches you how to make these joints and installations.

Clearly, cabinetwork goes more smoothly with a professional-quality table saw, a wide assortment of other woodworking tools, and a spacious workshop. But this book is not written for the well-tooled woodworker. We will show you how to make crisp, tight joints using a circular saw or a handsaw. It's a good idea to "earn" any upgrade in tools: Build some projects using modest tools, and buy more expensive equipment only after you decide that you want to tackle and complete more complex projects.

Roughly half the book is devoted to teaching you skills that can be applied to any cabinet and shelf project. With these skills under your belt, you can design a project custom-made for any space. The instructions for the specific projects in the second half of the book use the skills taught in the first half.

This is a cabinet and shelf book intended for do-it-yourselfers, not a furniture-making book or a manual for those who aspire to be fine craftsmen. You won't find information on making the fine joints found on expensive, handmade furniture. The goal is to show you the easiest and most efficient way to make high-quality cabinets and shelves.

How to Use This Book

Look through the "Tools and Materials" and "Basic Skills" sections. If there are skills unfamiliar to you there, read the appropriate sections. Browse through the projects shown on *pages 52–107* to see which projects interest you. When you choose a project, read all the way through its instructions before beginning work so that you will be familiar with all the tools, materials, and skills required.

If a project calls for a technique that you are not familiar with, read the section earlier in the book that gives instructions for it. Practice the technique on scrap pieces of wood until you feel confident; doing this may prevent you from ruining an expensive board or two.

Feature Boxes

In addition to regular instructions, the book is sprinkled with tips. For every project, a "You'll Need" box tells you how long the project will take, what skills are necessary, and what tools you must have. Other tip boxes pop up from time to time, providing practical help to ensure that your project will be as pleasurable as possible and that it will feature tight joints and long-lasting materials.

TOOLS TO USE

The right tools help make precise cuts and tight joints. If you need special tools not commonly found in a homeowner's toolbox, we'll tell you about them in Tools to Use.

Money $ Saver

Throwing money at a job does not necessarily make it a better one. Money Saver helps cut your costs with tips on how to estimate your material needs accurately, make wise tool purchases, and organize the job to minimize wasted labor.

CAUTION!

When a how-to step requires special care, Caution! warns you what to watch out for. It will help keep you from doing damage to yourself or the job at hand.

MEASUREMENTS

Cabinetry calls for precise measuring and marking. This box will help you when critical tolerances or special measuring techniques are called for.

EXPERTS' INSIGHT

Tricks of the trade can make all the difference in helping you do a job quickly and well. Experts' Insight gives you insiders' tips on how to make the job easier.

CABINETS AND SHELVES IN FAMILY SPACES

Plan storage units carefully so you will use every available inch of space. When you are in doubt about the future uses of your shelving units, use hardware to make them adjustable (see pages 54–57).

You may want to make your cabinet or shelf unit stand out visually; but usually it is more pleasing to have it blend in with its surroundings, so use moldings that match pieces in the room. If an exact duplicate is not available, you may be able to stack two or more moldings to get something very similar in appearance.

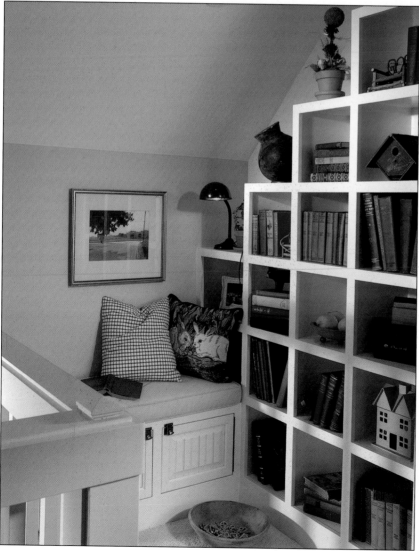

Low-tech storage for high-tech toys.
Painted bead board doors, flush rather than overlaid (see page 79), lend a rustic charm to this entertainment area (*above*). Make them by cutting and assembling the tongue-and-groove bead board, then screwing three braces to the back. A tape organizer like this can be bought and fitted into a custom unit. Small details have a large effect: Note the touch of color in the drawers and knobs.

Floor-to-ceiling books.
A small area—here, an overlook at the top of a stairway (*left*)—can be made into a hideaway for bookworms, with a cushioned bench and a straightforward set of shelves. The bench is similar to the window seat shown on pages 102–103. Topped with a cushion and some pillows, it need be no more complicated than a flat surface, about 15 inches high and 12–16 inches deep. The storage space underneath makes it easy for kids to put toys away. The shelves, a gridwork of squares, follow the slope of the ceiling. To get this effect, make plans on a piece of graph paper; the cubes must be just the right size.

A wall of shelves.

Repeated rectangular shapes are easy on the eye; the contents of the shelves take center stage. If you make shelves 12 inches high and 11 inches deep, most books will stand upright; magazines and coffee-table books can lie on their sides and you'll be able to incorporate some of your favorite art pieces. This unit (*above*) uses 1-by lumber or plywood for the shelves. Cut, fasten, and paint carefully to get a seamless look.

Trimmed-out overhead shelves.

Adding moldings to shelves gives them a richly textured appearance. The wider and more complex the molding, the richer the look. This set of adjustable shelves (*right*) is trimmed in rectangular sections with door casing. Wide crown molding at the top adds a classic touch. (See page 16 for information on molding.) Purchase short lengths of several moldings, and hold them against your shelves in different combinations to find the look that you want.

SPACE-MAXIMIZING CABINETS AND SHELVES

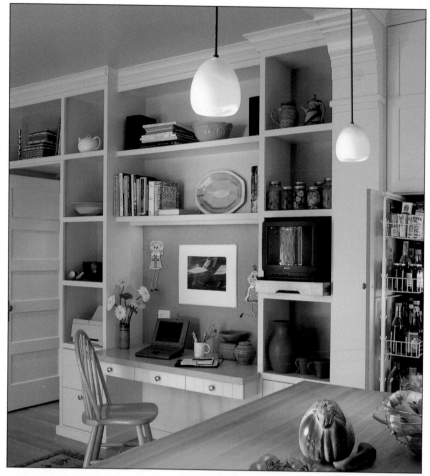

Kitchen desk area.

If you spend much time reading recipes, making shopping lists, and even paying bills in the kitchen, why not have a well-organized and comfortable desk, complete with drawers and shelves? This handsome unit (*left*) uses the same colors and hardware as the rest of the kitchen, but it features open shelves for storage and display. Moldings add interest, and high-gloss paint makes shelves nearly as washable as a countertop.

Stock and trade.

The deep neutral color of this strictly business home office (*below*) makes everything on the shelves come to life—from the simple geometry of books and magazines to the curves and warm tones of the baskets. The clean lines of the desk match the high-tech look of the wall of shelves, creating a complete, custom look for the whole room.

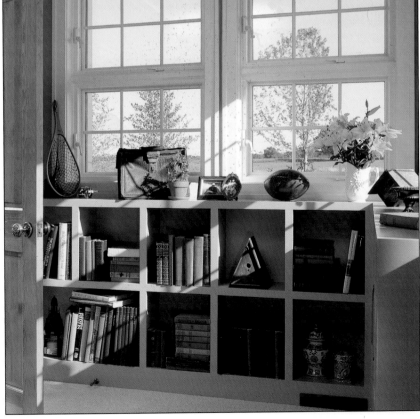

Hanging shelves.

Standards can be hung from the ceiling if you need open space under the shelves. This custom unit (*above*) is actually made of easily found materials: The shelves are MDF (see page 14), and the countertop was used as a template. After the edges were sanded smooth, several coats of polyurethane were applied. The hanging standards are aluminum fence posts attached to the ceiling.

Open cabinets down and around.

Simple, open cabinets with fixed shelves running along the wall (*right*) make efficient use of space behind the door and under the windows. This smart use of often-wasted space adds both storage and style to the room. The perpendicular cabinet makes a neat room divider and adds counter space, too.

HARD-WORKING CABINETS AND SHELVES

Shelves for baskets.

If you need stored items to be portable, there's no need to build elaborate removable drawers. Buy some attractive baskets (*left*), then build shelves designed to hold them comfortably. Make the fit loose enough to be able to see inside the baskets and remove them easily. These are attractively tagged, making it easy to keep track of kitchen linens.

Sewing closet.

A standard 24-inch-deep closet (*below*) is just right for a modest sewing area, with plenty of room for drawers and shelves to hold fabric, notions, and other miscellaneous items. When you're through sewing for the day, simply move the chair out of the way and close the doors.

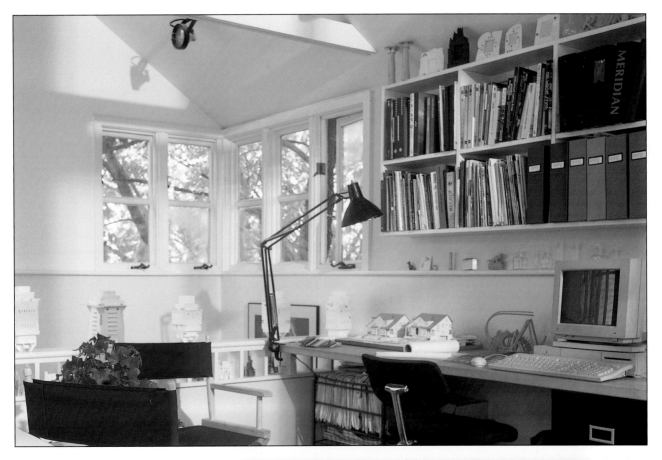

Floating shelves.

Shelves that hang with no visible means of support lend a subtly magical feel to a room. The "big box" (*above*) makes this designer's lode of publications float lightly on the wall within easy reach. Build the box, or boxes, then attach to the wall with angle brackets and screws driven into studs. For another type of floating shelves, see page 58.

Bathroom niche.

It's almost a given that every bathroom is short on storage and tight on space. The solution at (*right*) reclaims the open space within a stud wall. Neatly trimmed out with molding and painted to blend in the room, the niche adds and elegant touch and plenty of display space. And the room feels just that much larger. For other niche options, see pages 69-70.

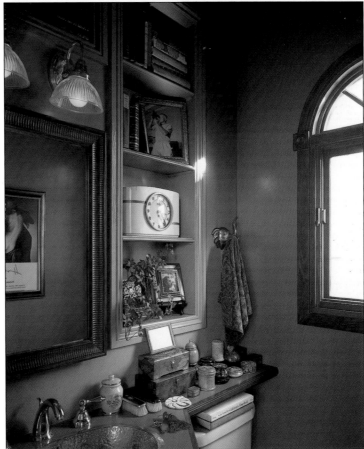

SELECTING LUMBER

Lumber for cabinets and shelves (often called "millwork lumber") is held to higher standards than wood used for general construction (known as "dimensional lumber"). It generally has tightly spaced grain lines and few or no knots. The edges have fairly sharp corners. Find a lumber supplier that stores millwork lumber laid flat in a protected area so that it is not warped. Even if you will be painting your project, choose each board very carefully, looking at each surface as well as sighting down its length. A slight **bow** or **crook** and some **twists** can be straightened as you fasten the board. A **cupped** board can be straightened only if you drive fasteners along its width. A tight **knot** is only a cosmetic problem; a loose knot may fall out. **Checking** is a surface problem, but a **split** cannot be repaired and will probably grow.

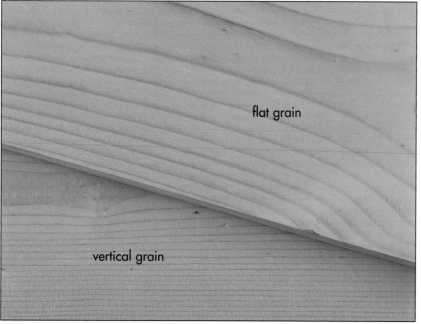

Vertical and flat grain.
Depending on how a board is cut from the log, it will have vertical grain, with narrow, closely spaced grain lines, or flat grain, with wavy, widely spaced lines. Many boards are a combination of the two. Vertical-grain wood is stronger and less likely to warp than flat-grain wood. So choose boards with narrow lines whenever possible.

COMMON GRADES OF LUMBER

Wood grading systems can vary depending on the species, the manufacturer, and even the lumberyard. Here are some common grades:

■ The best grades of hardwood are "firsts" and "seconds"; FAS combines them; they are clear or nearly clear. "Select" boards have small knots on one side only. No. 1 and 2 common boards have more noticeable knots.

■ The best softwoods are classified "select." Grade A select is clear, with no knots or blemishes. B, C, and D select have increasingly more and larger knots and blemishes. For shelving that will be painted, or for a rustic look, use No. 2 common.

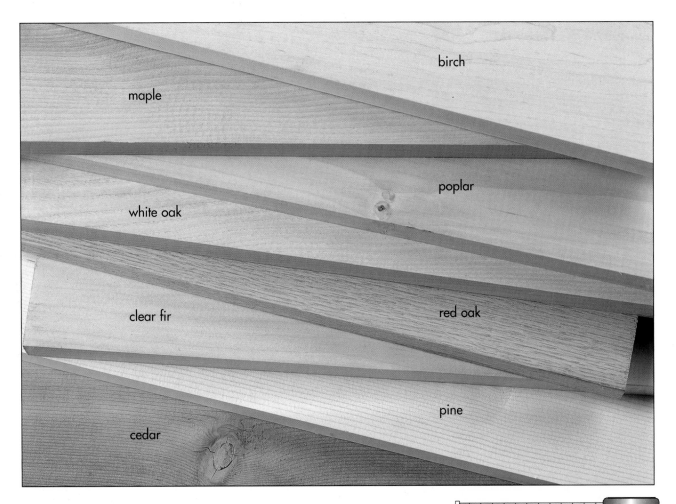

maple
birch
white oak
poplar
clear fir
red oak
pine
cedar

Wood species.

Hardwood comes from deciduous trees that grow slowly, making the lumber hard and durable and often very expensive. Although it is often available in standard sizes (see chart *right),* sometimes it is milled to odd widths to make use of as much wood as possible. If the boards are smoothed on only two sides (S2S), the edges will be too rough and uneven to use, so have the yard mill the edges.

Maple is extremely hard and difficult to cut. It is usually very light in color but can be reddish. **Red oak,** which is actually reddish brown, has a distinctive open grain; it resists warping but may shrink. **White oak's** grain is not quite so pronounced. It is lighter and more consistent in color than red oak, as well as more resistant to shrinking. **Birch** is similar in appearance and hardness to maple, and it is less expensive.

Poplar is the lightest, softest, and least expensive of these hardwoods. The grain of poplar is not especially pretty, so it's a good choice for pieces that will be painted or for areas that will not be visible.

Softwood, which comes from coniferous trees, not only is softer but has a more casual appearance than hardwood. Use it for projects that will not receive much direct contact; even if painted, it can be easily dented.

Pine is very light and soft, making it easy to work with but weak. It resists warping but is prone to shrinkage. **Fir** is the strongest and heaviest of the softwoods listed here. Clear fir is a good choice for outdoor furniture. **Cedar** is extremely soft, with a distinctive cream-to-brown color. Use aromatic red cedar for a pleasant smell and resistance to moth infestation.

MEASUREMENTS

LUMBER SIZES

A board that was 2 inches thick and 4 inches wide when cut is called a 2×4. But due to shrinkage and milling, the board you buy will be $1\frac{1}{2}$ inches by $3\frac{1}{2}$ inches. "2×4" is the *nominal* size; the true dimensions are the *actual* size. Here are some of the most common sizes:

Nominal Size	Actual Size
1×2	$\frac{3}{4}$" × $1\frac{1}{2}$"
1×4	$\frac{3}{4}$" × $3\frac{1}{2}$"
1×6	$\frac{3}{4}$" × $5\frac{1}{2}$"
1×8	$\frac{3}{4}$" × $7\frac{1}{4}$"
1×10	$\frac{3}{4}$" × $9\frac{1}{4}$"
1×12	$\frac{3}{4}$" × $11\frac{1}{4}$"
2×2	$1\frac{1}{2}$" × $1\frac{1}{2}$"
2×6	$1\frac{1}{2}$" × $5\frac{1}{2}$"

CHOOSING SHEET GOODS

You can create large surfaces easily and inexpensively with sheet goods. However, the edges will have to be covered, and the surface will rarely be good-looking enough to stain.

Plywood has great strength and resistance to cracking because it is made from layers of veneer with grains running in opposite directions. Softwood plywood is the most common, but you can buy sheets with veneers made of almost any kind of hardwood.

Hardboard is the least expensive of these sheet goods. Tempered hardboard is water-resistant, but it will puff up and weaken if it gets soaked. Perforated hardboard ("pegboard") is a quick shop storage option.

Particleboard is made of glued sawdust and very small chips, making it hard but it's easily broken. Use it as a substrate for laminate.

Medium-density fiberboard (MDF) uses even finer wood fiber to create a smooth and workable surface. It can be sanded smooth. Painted, it makes a serviceable and fairly strong finished surface. However, like particleboard, it can easily split when nails or screws are driven through it. Both of these products expand and weaken if they become wet.

Particleboard or MDF can be covered with **melamine,** a thin layer of plastic. Use melamine board for cabinet and shelf parts that will not get bumped much.

Wafer board is made of wood chips glued together in a random pattern. **Oriented-strand board** (OSB) arranges the chips so they run in one direction for one layer, then at right angles for the next layer. OSB is nearly as strong as plywood. Both have rough surfaces and should be used only where they will not be visible, or for utility or shop shelving.

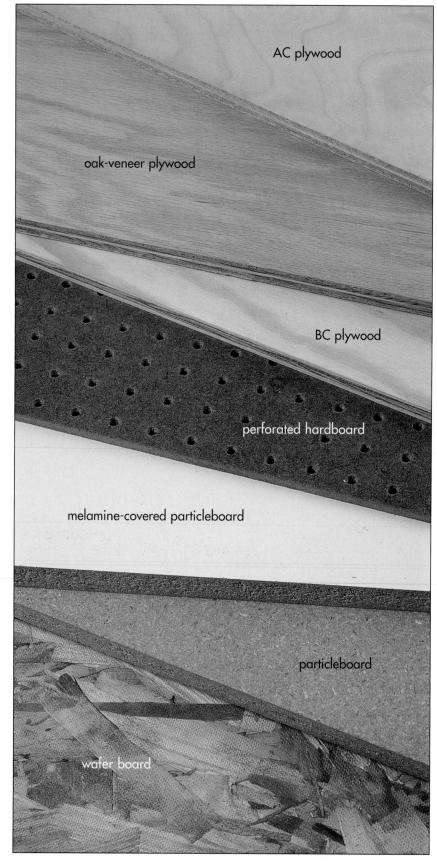

oak-veneer plywood

AC plywood

BC plywood

perforated hardboard

melamine-covered particleboard

particleboard

wafer board

EXPERTS' INSIGHT

ADVANTAGES OF HARDWOOD PLYWOOD

Oak plywood, and plywood made of other hardwood, can be stained an attractive color. However, the grain lines are usually very wide, making for an appearance that is very different from millwork lumber.

There are two good reasons for using birch plywood—usually the least expensive hardwood plywood—even when you are going to paint it. First, it is much harder than standard softwood plywood, which dents very easily. Second, birch and other hardwoods soak up less paint, requiring fewer coats of paint.

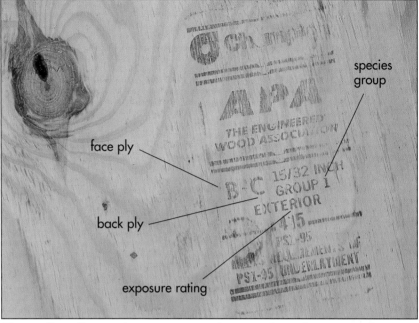

Plywood grading.

The large letters on a softwood plywood grading stamp indicate the face grades. An "A" surface has no knots; a "B" face has only small, tight knots; "C" and "D" sides have progressively larger knots and rougher grain. This sheet has one "B" side and one "C" side. If the stamp says "Group 1," it uses a wood species rated the strongest; "Group 2" is less strong. An "exterior" rating means that it will resist moisture well.

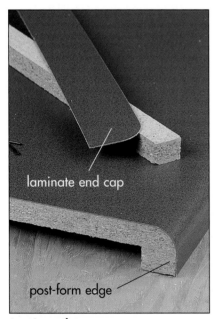

Laminated countertop.

Countertops usually have a sheet of hard plastic laminated to particleboard. You can make your own square-edged top by attaching plastic laminate to particleboard with contact cement. A post-form top has rounded edges and must be factory-made.

Plywood defects.

A plywood face is rarely perfect, but better surfaces have been repaired more skillfully. The best surfaces use small pieces of repair wood that match the surrounding area so they are barely noticed. Lower-grade surfaces use large plugs, sometimes in the shape of footballs and often are clearly different from their surroundings. If you are going to paint, make sure that the patch feels smooth.

Gaps along the edge should be filled with wood putty, or else the edge will be easily damaged. If an area feels softer than the surrounding area, it is hollow.

SELECTING MOLDINGS

Nothing spruces up a plain piece of cabinetry quicker than a piece of molding. Home centers have a large selection of profiles to choose from. Most are designed for a specific purpose—baseboard for the bottom of a wall, casing for around doors, and so on. But you can use them any way you want. By stacking moldings, or positioning them next to each other, you can create a custom look.

Standard profile moldings are available in random lengths ranging from 4 to 20 feet. Whenever possible, order pieces long enough to span the entire distance; butt joints are surprisingly hard to get perfect. It is worth your while to measure for each piece and make a list. Buy just the sizes you need, adding a few inches extra for each piece.

Carved and embossed moldings come in set lengths. Often they are worth the steep price, because a few pieces can have a dramatic effect on your project.

Pine molding is the most common. If you will be painting, primed molding—perhaps made of MDF (see page 14)—may be cheaper and will be easier to paint. Oak molding can lend a classy look: make sure the grain and color match the wood it will abut. Paper-covered hardboard molding does not cut cleanly, making it difficult to make a tight joint.

It may be difficult to find a factory piece to match the profile of an older molding. However, some lumberyards or wood shops will custom-mill molding for you. It may be worth the extra cost and trouble to get just the molding you want.

Use a router to cut a molding profile on a piece of wood. There is a wide variety of router bits; these can be set at various depths and used in combination to make unique edge profiles.

Finger-jointed molding.
These inexpensive moldings use short pieces joined together end-to-end. As long as the joints are smooth (feel them to be sure), they will paint as well as standard molding; however, the finger joint will show through stain.

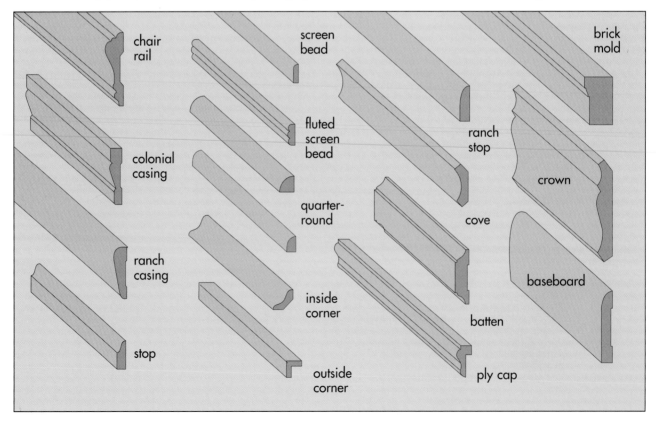

chair rail

colonial casing

ranch casing

stop

screen bead

fluted screen bead

quarter-round

inside corner

outside corner

ranch stop

cove

batten

ply cap

brick mold

crown

baseboard

STORING LUMBER

*T*rees are rarely straight, so it is in the nature of wood to twist. That is why even the best lumber will warp eventually if it is not stacked properly. And don't be surprised if a lesser-quality board develops serious waves in a day or two.

Boards in good lumberyards are always laid flat and kept tightly stacked against each other. You'll see lots of S-shaped pieces at home centers where boards or molding is stored upright.

Plan a wood storage area that can accommodate boards and sheets of various sizes and puts them within easy reach. Humidity causes warping, so use a cool, dry place if possible. Keep all wood off bare concrete floors, especially if there is the possibility of occasional flooding.

The best way to store sheet goods is to lay them flat. However, this takes up space and makes it difficult to get at the board on the bottom of the pile, so set them on end. To minimize bowing, stand them as close to upright as possible, and place narrower pieces on the outside.

Store long boards close to eye level so you can see each board's dimension by looking at the end. Use several racks so you don't have tall stacks of boards. Perhaps assign one rack to molding, one to boards 1×4 and smaller, and one to wider boards.

Small pieces often come in handy when building cabinets. So set aside space for a variety of lengths and widths in your storage area. Provide a place for 4-foot-tall cutoffs from sheet goods. Also have several shelves for boards that are 4 feet or shorter in length.

When you stack the lumber, push all the pieces tightly against each other. Place the widest boards at the bottom, and stack progressively narrower boards as you go up the racks.

Sometimes the correct storage method can straighten a warped board. Set it on a flat surface, stack a board of the same size or larger on top of it, and place weights on top of both. In a month or so you should have a straight board.

molding
1×4s or smaller
lumber
large sheet goods (more than 4' long)
about 4'4"
6' to 8'
about 4'4"
small sheet goods (4' or shorter)

CHOOSING FASTENERS AND HARDWARE

For most cabinetwork, use **finish** nails or **trim head** screws. Use a **casing** nail if the head will be exposed to moisture; a **wire brad** when attaching thin moldings. **Corrugated fasteners** work only as temporary fasteners. To build heavy frameworks, **cement-coated** nails hold better than **common** or **box** nails. **Drywall** screws are called "all-purpose" because they are used for fastening most interior projects. Use a **trim head** screw for finish work. A **flathead** screw is driven flush with the surface; **ovalhead** and **roundhead** screws protrude. For finish work, combine a flathead screw with a **trim washer**. Use **masonry** screws when attaching frames to concrete or brick. For the strongest joints, drill holes and install **bolts**, **lag** screws, or **hanger** screws.

Mending plates and angle brackets.
Use these only for areas that will not be visible. They provide a quick way to fastening and are best for reinforcing joints, rather than being the only means of support. Clamp the boards together while you fasten. Drill a pilot hole and fasten one screw so it holds the metal piece in place. Then drill the rest of the pilot holes and drive those screws.

Catches.
Each type of catch has a different feel, so choose one type and use it for all the cabinets in one area. If used constantly, catches may need to be replaced after about five years. **Friction** and **roller** catches are quiet and inexpensive, but are the least durable. **Magnetic** catches close with a click. **Touch** catches are also magnetic and make pulls unnecessary.

Choose cabinet hardware.

Before choosing a hinge type, decide whether your cabinet will have flush or overlapped doors and whether the cabinet will be framed or frameless. Most cabinet doors are *overlapped*: They are larger than the opening and so overlap the cabinet opening by a half inch or so all around. This makes them easier to build and install than *flush* doors, which sit inside the opening and must fit perfectly or the gap between door and cabinet will be uneven. *Lipped* doors have rabbeted edges that overlap the opening. (A **sliding track** needs no hinges.) Framed cabinets use vertical and horizontal pieces, usually of 1×2 or 1×3, to provide rigidity. Frameless cabinets are sleeker in appearance and must use **Euro-style** or **wraparound** hinges.

The most common types of hinges are shown at right. (A bird's-eye view shows how they attach.) For a framed cabinet, the simplest configuration has an overlaid door and **semi-concealed** hinge. Square-cut the door to an inch larger than the opening, attach the hinges to the door, position the door, and attach the hinges to the frame. Lipped doors require **offset** hinges. To make sure they fit, buy the hinges before you cut the rabbet. For a flush door, use a **butt** hinge, a smaller version of a house door hinge. **Pivot** hinges require a V-shaped mortise in the top and bottom of the door. A **concealed** hinge can't be seen when the door is closed.

Frameless cabinets use Euro-style hinges that fit into holes in both the door and cabinet. With a Forstner bit (which bores a very clean hole), this is not difficult to do. These hinges have a big advantage: You can adjust them with a screwdriver to bring all your doors into alignment with each other. Adjusting the other hinges requires moving screws over—a more difficult task.

offset hinge — lipped door

butt hinge — flush door

wraparound hinge for lipped door

semi-concealed hinge — overlapped door

cylinder-style

Euro-style

pivot hinge

sliding track

wraparound hinge

wire pull

knob

CHOOSING HAND TOOLS

Accurate, sharp, and comfortable tools make working with wood a pleasure; shoddy or ill-maintained tools turn it into a tiresome chore. Hand tools are less expensive than power tools, so don't hesitate to buy a hand tool when a project calls for it.

Keep your tools where you can find them easily and where they won't be damaged. If you have a shop, hang tools on pegboard hooks to keep them safe and handy. An inexpensive nylon-fabric insert for a 5-gallon bucket is a great way to haul hand tools. A leather tool pouch will make you feel like a real carpenter and puts the most-used tools within easy reach: knife, tape measure, chalk line, speed square, hammer, chisel, nail set, and screwdriver. Make a habit of putting these tools in the same holsters, and you'll be quick on the draw.

A 25-foot **tape measure** with a 1-inch-wide blade will handle most measuring jobs. (The hook at its end slides back and forth the same distance as its thickness to give an accurate measurement whether hooking it on the end of a board or butting it up against a surface.)

With a **chalk line**, you can make perfectly straight lines over long distances. Have plenty of pencils on hand; they have a habit of getting lost. A **speed square** is sturdy, so it is easy to use as a guide for square circular-saw cuts and is not easily knocked out of alignment. Use a **T-bevel** to transfer odd angles. For checking large objects for square, or for drawing long square lines, a **framing square** (carpenter's square) is indispensible. Buy a **level** to check for plumb.

A **backsaw with miter box** enables you to make accurate square and 45-degree cuts in

moldings and small boards. A **coping saw** is necessary to make coped cuts in molding (see page 30). Use a **drywall saw** or **keyhole saw** to make rough cuts in walls or boards, which are sometimes needed when installing cabinets. Have a **caulking gun** ready for applying adhesive.

Shave a board smoothly with an accurately adjusted **plane** that has a sharp blade. Sandpaper on a **sanding block** will complete the job. A **Surform** tool (rasping plane) takes less skill to use but produces a rough surface. Use a **rasp** to shape small areas. A **utility knife** comes in handy for trimming splinters and rough ends and for making precise measuring marks. Buy one with a retractable blade or reserve a pocket in your leather pouch for a knife with a fixed blade. **Chisels** are needed for mortising; have at least two sizes—½ inch and 1 inch.

You will need **phillips-head** and **slot-head screwdrivers**—at least two sizes of each. A combination screwdriver has four tips and is easier to keep track of than four screwdrivers. Use an **awl** to make starter holes for small screws.

Tongue-and-groove pliers grip objects of various sizes and give you plenty of leverage. **Locking pliers** keep a tight grip while you work with two hands. Use an **adjustable (crescent) wrench** to tighten and loosen bolts and nuts. A good selection of **clamps** (see pages 34–35) will enable you to firmly glue together many cabinet projects and damaged furniture.

You'll use your **hammer** often, so choose one that is comfortable. A 16-ounce one with curved claws is the most popular choice. Buy variously sized **nail sets** so you can set and countersink small and large finish nails. A **pry bar** is indispensible for demolition.

chalk line

awl

adjustable clamp

level

spring clamp

C-clamp

tape measure

nail set

framing square

T-bevel

speed square

drywall saw

caulking gun

keyhole saw

pry bar

backsaw

phillips-head screwdriver

slot-head screwdriver

coping saw

miter box

tongue-and-groove pliers

hammer

utility knife

adjustable wrench

block plane

chisel

Surform tool

locking pliers

rasp

SELECTING POWER TOOLS

You can make shelves and straightforward cabinets using the same tools you need for house repairs and remodeling. The basic trio of circular saw, drill, and saber saw will equip you to cut most any line, bore any hole, and quickly drive screws.

For all the tools shown on these two pages, amperage rather than horsepower is an indication of power. A tool with ball bearings will make work more pleasant.

A carpenter uses a **circular saw** constantly. It crosscuts, rips boards lengthwise, and makes miter and beveled cuts. A high-quality circular saw used with a guide will make shop-quality cuts. When shopping, look for a saw that pulls at least 12 amps and that uses ball bearings—a combination that will make for smooth cuts and long life. When you turn on the motor, it should run smoothly, and there should be absolutely no wobble in the blade. The baseplate should be at least $1/16$ inch thick. A saw with a $7\frac{1}{4}$-inch blade is a good all-purpose tool. For cabinetwork, consider buying a smaller, lighter model. Use a hollow-ground planer blade or a plywood blade when you need precise cuts.

A variable-speed, reversible **power drill** with a $3/8$-inch chuck is essential for carpenter and woodworker alike. It should pull at least 3.5 amps. A keyless chuck allows you to change bits very quickly, but it's hard for some people to adequately tighten the bits. Use one if you have strong hands.

A **cordless drill** is a wonderful convenience. Buy one that uses at least 12 volts. A second battery pack is a must.

Maintain a complete selection of twist bits, from $1/16$ to $1/4$ inch in diameter. Brad-point bits cut cleaner holes than standard twist bits. For larger holes, use inexpensive spade bits, hole saws, or, for the cleanest cuts, Forstner bits.

Choose a **saber saw** that pulls at least 3 amps. The baseplate should be at least $1/16$ inch thick. Make sure that the angle-adjusting mechanism is easy to use and makes it possible to tighten the baseplate securely in any position.

cordless drill

power drill

saber saw

circular saw

Variable speed gives you more control over your cuts. A scrolling knob allows you to make turns without having to get into awkward positions.

Some tools are not used often but are essential on occasion. If you seldom use them, settle for a less expensive tool or rent a professional-quality tool.

A **router** allows you to make mill lumber edges to almost any shape; a vast variety of router bits is available (see page 31). The best way to get clean, even cuts is to set the router in a router table. Guides can be nearly as accurate. A self-piloted bit, which has rollers that run along the edge it is cutting, can make straight cuts, but only if the edge it is rolling against is perfectly straight.

With a **biscuit joiner**, you can quickly join pieces edge to edge.

The faces of the pieces will be perfectly flush with each other. You will need to glue and clamp the pieces (see page 37).

A **power miter saw**, also called a chop saw or cutoff saw, easily makes accurate crosscuts and miter cuts. A model using a 10-inch blade will miter-cut boards up to 2×6. Pay extra for a compound miter saw only if you anticipate projects calling for compound miter cuts. A thin-kerf carbide-tipped blade with at least 40 teeth will cut cleanly and last a long time.

A **belt sander** will quickly smooth—and plane away—material from a large area. It should be fairly heavy and have a dust collector. Check that it uses a belt size that is commonly available: 3×24 and 3×21 inches are popular. Maintain a selection

of belts of at least three grits. If you have belts of 50, 80, and 120 grit, you will be able to both remove material quickly and bring a surface to a fairly smooth finish. A belt sander has definite limitations, however. Unless used carefully, it can quickly and surprisingly dig gouges in wood. Use the belt sander for rough work, and finish by sanding by hand or using a vibrating or random-orbit sander.

A **random-orbit sander** works by moving in small circles, rather than just vibrating. It removes material more quickly than an older vibrating sander, but some people feel the resulting finish is not as smooth. If you need to sand in tight spots, a detail sander is a good investment. Have a variety of sandpapers on hand ranging from 80 grit to 320 grit.

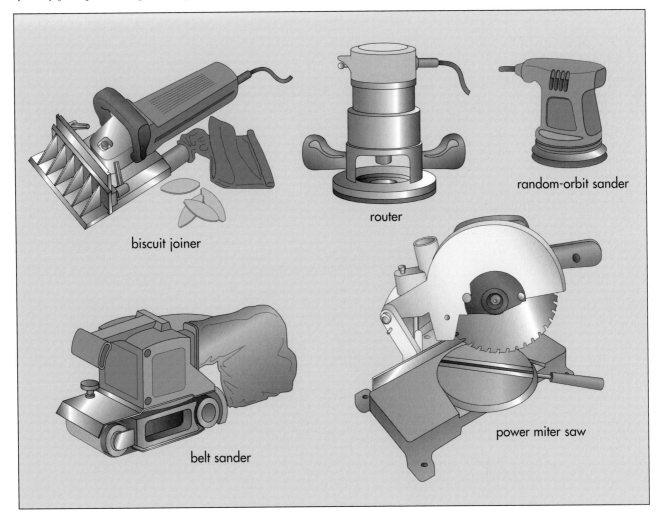

biscuit joiner

router

random-orbit sander

belt sander

power miter saw

CHOOSING SHOP TOOLS

A shop is a must for a cabinetmaker. It need not be large or elaborate; but without a well-organized, brightly lit, and comfortable place to work, building will be a struggle and results may be disappointing.

■ The first thing you need is a work surface. It must be flat and even and large enough to hold your projects; otherwise, it will be hard to build things that are square in both directions. You could work on the floor, but that will get tiresome in a hurry as you will be on your knees. A simple 8-foot by 3-foot workbench, 40 inches tall and made of ¾-inch plywood and 2×4s, makes a fine worktable.

■ Place stationary power tools so that you can easily position wood on them. For a table saw or radial-arm saw, you must be able to slide full 4×8 sheets of plywood all the way through. Position your workbench or other supporting structure so that the plywood sheets have a surface to rest on.

■ Provide plenty of light, directed so your body won't make shadows while you work. Large fluorescent fixtures work best.

■ Place 20-amp electrical receptacles in convenient places so you won't have a tangle of extension cords. For a shop with several power tools, consider putting in a separate circuit.

■ Make it easy to clean your shop—and to keep dust from filtering into the rest of the house. Place a large garbage can where you can toss scraps of wood right after cutting. Use dust bags on power tools whenever possible. Keep a workshop vac plugged in and within easy reach. An exhaust fan—even a box fan placed in a window—will blow fine dust out of the room. The best and most expensive solution is a central dust collector with tubes running to all the power tools.

■ Keep your hand tools in sight and within easy reach. A sheet of perforated hardboard (pegboard), attached to 1×2 furring strips on the wall, is a time-tested method. If tool hooks pop out too easily, glue them in place with construction adhesive.

■ Provide storage for lumber (see page 17) and for fasteners and other hardware. Store nails and screws on shelves. Use labels to mark their sizes so you don't have to dig through them to find the screw you want.

Consider attaching jar lids to an overhead surface so that you can unscrew a glass jar full of nails or screws with one hand.

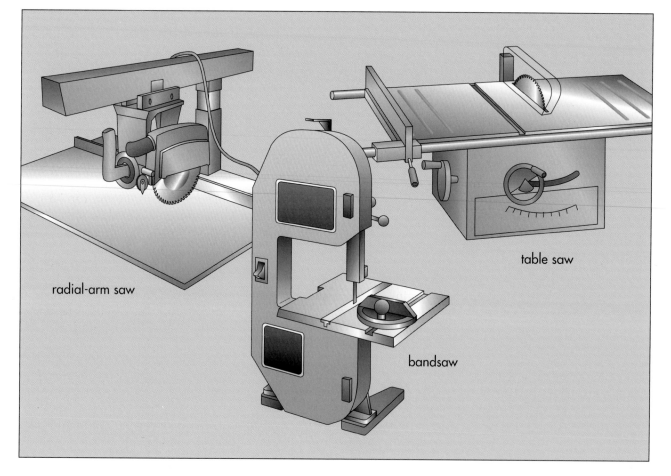

radial-arm saw

bandsaw

table saw

carpenter's vise

drill press

tabletop vise

grinder

A **table saw** (see pages 28–29 and 40–41) can handle most cutting and grooving jobs and will be in use frequently. In fact, you may want to design your entire shop around it; it will be the workhorse of your shop.

Choose a table saw with a solid table that will not vibrate while you work. The rip fence is very important. It should stay firmly in place when clamped, align perfectly parallel to the blade, and be easy to move. The crosscutting guide should slide smoothly and easily in its groove.

The more powerful the motor, the better. A belt-driven model works more smoothly and lasts longer than a "motorized" model, which has the arbor attached directly to the motor.

Some portable (or benchtop) table saws can make accurate cuts, but a freestanding table saw will be worth the extra price in the long run. The most popular size that woodworkers use is a 10-inch blade. If you pay the extra money for a carbide-tipped combination blade with 40 or more teeth, you will be able to make splinter-free cuts for a long time before changing blades.

A 10-inch **radial-arm saw** is also an all-purpose tool, though you will find making long rip cuts easier with a table saw. Unless you buy the best quality model, its cuts will probably be slightly less precise than those made by a good table saw. Check to see that the motor glides easily and without wobbling during crosscuts. When clamped in position for a rip cut, it should be unshakable. See how long it takes you to switch from crosscut to miter, bevel, and rip cuts. The crank for raising and lowering the blade should operate easily.

Use a **bandsaw** to make scrollwork cuts in small pieces. A decent model will cost you about the same as a good saber saw, and it will be fun to use. You will sometimes be limited in the size of board you can cut; the saw arm may get in the way as you swing the board around. A heavy-duty model can be used to rip-cut or crosscut like a table saw.

You can bore accurate holes using a jig and a standard hand drill (see page 36), but a **drill press** makes it much easier. The table should tilt, for drilling at angles. See that the motor and bit move up and down without the slightest wobble, and that the table can be adjusted easily and clamped firmly in position.

A **bench grinder** is an expensive tool that also can be surprisingly handy. Use it to sharpen chisels and plane blades, as well as for a variety of household sharpening chores.

A standard **tabletop vise** is mounted with lag screws or bolts on top of the table, and is useful for holding a variety of objects. However, a **carpenter's vise** is better for most woodworking projects. It mounts to the side of the bench and the wider jaws clamp boards without denting them. (To make it even more dent-proof, mount pieces of wood on the inside of the jaws.)

USING A CIRCULAR SAW OR A SABER SAW

Begin cutting with a circular saw or a saber saw by placing the front of the baseplate on the board, and keep the blade back from the board. Pull the trigger and allow the motor to reach full speed, then push the blade into the cut. Focus your eyes on the blade as you cut, not the notch. Find the correct path and push through with a smooth stroke. Don't make small changes in direction as you cut. Before using your circular saw to make precise cuts with a guide, learn to use it as a general carpentry tool. Take some time to practice: Draw a series of square lines across a board, and slice through them one by one. Once you feel comfortable and can cut straight lines by hand, you'll be better prepared to use a guide. With a saber saw, make practice cuts until you can make both smooth curves and even straight cuts. Your first tries will no doubt go astray; keep on slicing until you get the knack.

Measure and mark.
Whenever possible, hold a board in the place where it will go and mark it, rather than using a tape measure. To pinpoint the cutoff spot, draw a **V** instead of a straight line; the tip marks the exact spot.

To make the cutoff line, hold the tip of the pencil on the tip of the **V**, and slide the square over to it. Draw the line, then mark an **X** where the waste will be so that you can be sure to cut on the correct side of the line.

Square the blade.
Before cutting, make sure that your blade is square; the guide on the saw may be inaccurate. Hold a speed square against the blade. To test, crosscut a 2×4. Flip one side over; if the cut edges meet perfectly, the blade is square.

Support the material.
A board that is not properly supported can bind the blade, causing the saw to kick back dangerously. If the scrap piece is short, support the board on the good side and let the scrap fall. Letting a longer scrap fall will produce splinters or cause binding, so support the board in four places. Make sure the two inner supports are not lower than the outer supports, or the board will bow downward and bind. You can cut the board roughly to size, then make the finish cut.

Bevel cut.
Circular saw bevel guides are often not reliable, so test on a scrap before making a cut. You can use a speed square or a T-bevel to check the blade. You may need to retract the blade guard—it could cause the cut to go astray. This is a difficult cut, so brace the board and use a clamped guide.

Long cut in sheet goods.
Support the sheet in four places so that after the cut is made, the two pieces will be stable. Measure the distance between the outside of the baseplate and the blade— keeping in mind which side of the line you want to cut—and clamp a straightedge as a guide. Don't press too hard against the guide.

Score across grain or veneer.
To make sure you do not produce splinters when cutting a veneer or cutting across the grain, use a knife and straightedge to score a line that is about $1/16$ inch above the cut line. When cutting a door or other object with thin veneer, knife-cut all the way through the veneer—it may take several passes.

Inside cut with saber saw.
When cutting out an area on the inside of a board, first bore at least one hole, large enough for the saber saw blade to fit in, inside the cut lines. When you cut with a saber saw, it is important to keep the baseplate flat on the board. Press down on the board with more pressure than you use for pushing forward.

Curved cuts.
To cut a long curve, make sure that the board is clamped tightly and that there are no obstructions to the cut under the board. Make sure that the baseplate thumbscrew is firmly tightened; wobbling is the most common cause of ugly saber saw cuts.

With practice, you can make cuts that are evenly arced. The trick is to turn the saw with steady consistency as you push forward at a constant speed. This produces a smoother cut than making frequent small corrections.

Move slowly without forcing the blade. Avoid sharp turns—that can easily break a blade. If you wander from the line, back up and try again. If the saw heats up or if you smell smoke, stop.

CUTTING WITH A TABLE AND RADIAL ARM SAW

The best way to ensure accurate table saw and radial arm saw cuts is to set up carefully. Make sure the blade is precisely square or beveled. See that the rip guide is perfectly parallel to the blade and that the miter gauge is at a perfect right angle or miter angle. Make test cuts on scrap pieces.

push stick

featherboard pushes work against fence

Rip cut.
Measure from the rip guide to the teeth of the blade. To be sure your cut will be accurate, make a cut in a scrap piece and measure it. Adjust the blade to ¼ inch above the top of the board. Start the motor and allow it to reach full speed. Hold the board so it glides smoothly and is tight against the fence at all points as you push it forward. Avoid stopping and starting as much as possible; that can make the cut irregular.

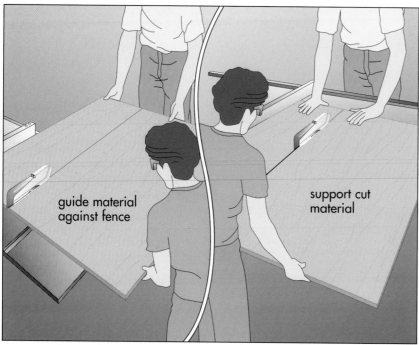

guide material against fence

support cut material

rip fence

Cutting a large sheet.
With practice and a good worktable beyond the saw, you can learn to cut full sheets by yourself. But it is safer to have a helper stand to the side to assist you in positioning the sheet up against the fence. Turn on the saw and push the sheet through, all the time making sure it is against the fence. Halfway through the cut, the helper should move behind the saw to support the portion of the sheet leaving the table.

Beveled rip cut.
It may be hard to get this aligned. After adjusting the bevel, hold the board against the rip fence and slide both of them until the blade lines up with the cut line. Make a small test cut first.

sandpaper attached so work won't slip

gauge with hold-down clamp

facing strip for crosscutting long material

gauge with stop rod attachment

miter gauge

cutting jig

Crosscut.

Slip the miter gauge (see the useful features at *right*) into its channel. Use the table to check for square. Set the blade depth to ¼ inch above the board and start the motor. Clasp the board to the gauge and slide it through the blade. Hold the board only on the gauge side of the blade; it will bind if you hold both sides.

Crosscutting identical lengths.

To cut a series of boards the same length, clamp a length of scrap onto the front end of the rip fence, and space it the length you want your pieces. Use the clamped scrap as a cutting jig to size each piece. Hold the pieces firmly as you slide them forward so that your cuts will be accurate. Or, you can use a stop rod attachment to do this.

pull slowly

anti-kickback mechanism

Crosscut or miter cut with a radial arm saw.

There is a tightening lever that must be loosened every time you change from crosscut to rip cut. If you don't tighten it again before making a cut, the blade will wobble. See that the board lies perfectly flat on the table. With the saw running, lower the blade so it cuts just below the surface. Hold the board flush against the fence, and pull slowly to make sure the blade hits the cut line exactly. Then pull the saw through in one motion. Pull slowly, especially if cutting 2-by lumber or hardwood; if you pull too fast, the saw will bind.

Rip-cutting.

For rip-cutting, the blade rotates up against the board—the opposite of a crosscut. For a beveled rip like the one shown, you will need to raise the blade as much as several inches before it can be positioned for the bevel. Start the motor with the blade slightly above the table, then lower it. Position the antikickback mechanism so it will grab the board if it starts to shoot backwards. If the motor stops midcut, shut it off immediately, pull the board back, and start again. If the motor overheats and turns itself off, wait a few minutes before you push the reset button.

CUTTING MOLDING

A miter joint is made of two pieces that are angle-cut or bevel-cut at the same angle and then joined together. Most often, two pieces cut to 45 degrees are joined to make a 90-degree corner. If miter cuts are off even half a degree, the joint will look sloppy.

An inexpensive plastic or wood miter box like the one at *right* can make accurate cuts, but you'll need to struggle a bit to achieve real precision. Another type of miter box uses what looks like a hacksaw running through a sliding mechanism; it will be more precise and easier to use. The easiest way to cut molding is with a power miter box (*below*).

Most mistakes occur not in the cutting but in the measuring. When possible, make the miter cut first, and hold the piece in the place it will go so you can mark for the straight cut at the other end. It's easy to get confused about the direction of the miter cut; hold the piece in place to be sure.

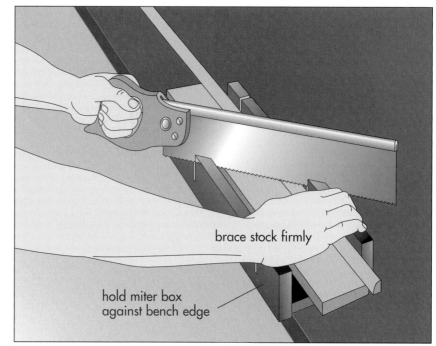

brace stock firmly

hold miter box against bench edge

Miter cutting by hand.
With a box like this one, place a scrap of 1×4 in the bottom so you can saw completely through the piece without cutting through the bottom of the miter box. To avoid confusion, place the board or molding in the position it will be when in use. Firmly clasp the piece up against the far side of the miter box. Start the cut slowly to make sure you are cutting on the right side of the line. Hold the piece tightly as you saw, or it may pop out.

Cutting with a power miter box.
Because the blade is round, the cut may begin not at the edge of the piece but in the middle; use a square to draw a cut line all the way across. Hold the piece firmly, and keep your hand well away from the blade. Start the motor and lower it slowly and steadily.

45°

coped end

straight cut against wall

Cutting for a coped joint.
At inside corners, simply bevel-cutting the two pieces may produce an imperfect joint, especially if the walls you're working with are out of square. Pros usually make a coped joint.

Cut the first piece square, and install it tightly against the wall.

Cut the second piece at a 45-degree miter cut, then use a coping saw to cut away the wood along the molding profile. Cut off a little more than needed to ensure a tight fit. When possible, cut the coped end first, then hold the molding in place and mark to cut the other end to the correct length.

USING A ROUTER

No tool gives you the power to shape wood like a router. By choosing a bit and setting it to the proper depth, you can produce a board edge or a groove that is unique. You may even save money by milling your own molding.

Piloted bits use the edge of the board as a guide; as long as the board is straight, the routed edge will be as well. When routing in the middle of a board with other bits, however, you will find that the router jerks in a counter-clockwise direction, making it hard to control. Use a clamped board (page 41) or a router guide (*below right*) to keep it from wandering. If you will be doing a lot of this type of work, consider buying a router table and mounting the router onto it. The table provides a flat work surface, as well as an adjustable fence for consistently accurate cuts.

cutting depth of router bit

wing nut

Adjusting the router.
Unplug the router and secure the bit in the chuck. To adjust the bit depth, loosen the router base around the motor. This involves turning a wing nut and adjusting the depth gauge on most models. Set the depth gauge at zero or so that the bit is even with the bottom of the base. Set the router on the edge of a table and lower the bit to the desired depth. Use the depth gauge or draw a line on the edge of the table indicating depth. Tighten the nut to secure the base. Test on a scrap board.

core-box | dado | straight cut | rabbet | flush-trim
dovetail | V-groove | plunge cut | corner-round | chamfer

Choosing bits.
Use a flush-trim bit, or one similar to it with a slight bevel, to finish the edges of a piece that has had a veneer of laminate glued to it. Rabbet, chamfer, and corner-round bits are all piloted. The ones shown have a wheel, running on ball bearings, that run along the edge of the board. Cheaper piloted bits don't have these wheels so they may burn the edge of the wood.

To use nonpiloted bits, a guide of some sort is necessary. Cut with two or more bits, slightly offset from each other, to make unique and intricate shapes.

Note: *Although you cannot see them while you are cutting, be aware that these bits are very sharp and are rotating at high speed. Keep your hands well away.*

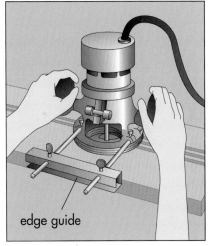

edge guide

Using a guide.
The guide above is only one of several types available. This one is an edge guide, designed to rout a channel parallel to the edge of the board. To cut circles or curves, use a trammel-point guide. Guides are also available for cutting dovetail joints and perfect hinge mortises. Once you've set up, you can make these intricate cuts quickly.

USING SIMPLE JOINERY

Making strong, tight wood joints is basic to cabinetmaking. On these pages we show some of the easiest methods.

Boards must be cut accurately in order to be joined tightly. Hone your measuring, marking, and cutting skills before tackling joinery, see pages 26–30.

When planning a cabinet or shelf project, always take into account the joinery technique. Often the joint you choose will determine the exact length of the boards. Perhaps the most common woodworking mistake is to get confused about which board overlaps which and cut them to wrong lengths.

Visualize how the joinery method will affect the final appearance. Perhaps the joint will be hidden. If the project will be painted, then driving screws or nails in visible places is not a problem. But if it will be stained, plug the hole to enhance the cabinet's appearance.

Butted ends.
The simplest way to build a carcass for a cabinet or shelves is to make standard 90-degree cuts. Most professionally made cabinets use simple butt joints.

Mitered ends.
For a more finished look, bevel-cut the ends so they meet in a miter joint. The wider the board, the more difficult it will be to get a perfect match.

Gluing.
Glue and nails work together to make a strong joint. Dry-fit the pieces, then apply an even bead of glue along the surface of one piece. If the wood is porous, brush glue onto both surfaces.

Driving and setting nails, screws.
Use clamps to hold the pieces together while you fasten them.

Soon after applying the glue, drill pilot holes and drive finish nails. Sink the heads beneath the surface with a nail set and fill the resulting hole with wood putty.

Trimhead screws will grab more tightly than nails, but they will leave larger holes to fill.

To keep the corner joints snug, drill diagonal holes and drive nails or screws through each joint.

TOOLS TO USE

MAGNETIC SLEEVE FOR A DRILL

Use this inexpensive tool to drive screws as quickly as you pound nails. The sleeve, which fits into the chuck of a drill, is magnetized so that any of the small bits you insert into the end will hold onto screw heads. The bits are inexpensive, so get a good selection. The No. 2 phillips bit will be used the most often. For trimhead screws you will need a No. 1 phillips bit. Add No. 2 and No. 1 slot bits, and you will be ready to drive almost any screw.

When using the bit, it usually works best to place the screw head onto the bit first; that way, you can drive shorter screws with one hand.

Countersinking and counterboring. A countersunk pilot hole will enable you to drive a screw head flush with the surface; a counterbored hole will let you sink the head. Combination drill bits do this quickly. Choose a bit that will allow the screw threads to grab without stressing the wood. To fill a counterbore, cut plugs out of a scrap of the same type of wood with a plug-cutting bit. Tap the plug into the hole with some glue, let dry, and sand smooth.

Hardware, wood reinforcement. The fasteners shown here can make a joint stronger or hold the pieces in place while you drill holes and drive dowels (see page 36). In casual settings that do not require a great deal of strength, they could work by themselves.

A simple **flat corner iron** can look dressy if you carefully mortise out the surrounding wood so that it sits perfectly flush. Small **wood blocks** add strength only if you drill pilot holes and fasten carefully so you don't split them. Take similar precautions when installing **corner braces** this close to the end of a board.

Plywood makes an excellent reinforcing material because it is so hard to split. A **plywood overlap** peppered with screws can add a surprising amount of strength; use this method where you will not see the plywood. A triangular **plywood gusset** adds rigidity.

GLUING AND CLAMPING

A joint that is glued without the use of fasteners can be stronger than the wood surrounding it. You must use the right glue, and you must clamp it firmly in place until the glue is completely set.

TOOLS TO USE

■ For most jobs where you join wood to wood, use woodworking (carpenter's) glue; it contains aliphatic resin, which makes it yellow. It is stronger and more resistant to heat than white polyvinyl resin glue and is worth the extra price. Some types are fast-drying, so you can remove the clamps in a half hour or so—but they take a full day to reach full strength.

■ Polyurethane glue is even stronger. It is impervious to moisture, making it ideal for outdoor projects. It foams up when it comes into contact with moisture so that it can fill in gaps. The foaming action means that if items are not tightly clamped, they will be pushed apart by the glue. It takes a full 24 hours for polyurethane glue to harden.

■ Epoxy glue comes in two parts that are mixed just before using. You can tightly glue almost any material with it, including metal and glass. Mixing and applying are time-consuming and awkward—you must spread it with a scrap of wood or cardboard.

■ Use construction adhesive to supplement the strength of fasteners. Buy it in caulking tubes for applying to small areas, or buy it in cans and spread with a notched trowel. Because it is thick, it doesn't run when applied to surfaces.

Gluing edge to edge.
Surprisingly, gluing pieces side by side provides a surface strong enough to use as a table. The edges must be perfectly straight, however, use a plane or have a shop smooth them with a jointer. Arrange the boards so the growth rings alternate (check the ends of the boards) to prevent the table from cupping with changes in humidity. Clamp very firmly.

Miter clamp.
Use this for mitered joints and for butt joints. It securely holds the pieces in perfect alignment while you fasten them.

Strap clamp.
This will allow you to glue several joints at once when assembling or repairing furniture, for instance.

EXPERTS' INSIGHT

CONTACT CEMENT

This allows you to tightly glue together large areas without clamping, but it is difficult to work with. It is commonly used to glue plastic laminate to particleboard to make a countertop. To do this, cut the laminate larger than needed. Coat both surfaces with contact cement, using a throwaway brush or roller. Place the laminate carefully—once placed, it cannot be budged. Use a roller to make sure it sticks everywhere. Finish the edges with a router or a file and sanding block.

Squeeze clamps.
These don't grab as securely as other clamps, but they are quick. Use for light clamping or to hold a straightedge guide for cutting.

Handscrew clamps.
With jaws made of wood, these are less likely than other clamps to dent the pieces. Use them to clamp pieces at almost any angle.

SQUARING A CABINET

When building cabinet and shelf units, keep your speed square and framing square handy so you can be vigilant about checking for square. If you drive fasteners while the pieces are out of square, you must remove the fasteners, square up the pieces, and drill new pilot holes for fasteners. (If you use the old holes, the fasteners will pull the pieces out of square.) Square cabinets begin with square cuts. Don't trust factory-cut ends of boards to be square (although sheet goods are trustworthy); every once in a while one is slightly off. Check each end with a speed square before you measure for cutting. Constantly checking for square can make it difficult to assemble cabinets, so consider making yourself a jig. This can be as simple as two pieces of 1×3 attached to your workbench, perfectly square and straight. You can then hold the pieces tight against the 1×3s as you fasten.

Use a piece of plywood.
You can't trust boards to be square, but sheet goods with factory edges make excellent squares. One very simple way to ensure square is to attach a piece of plywood or hardboard backing.

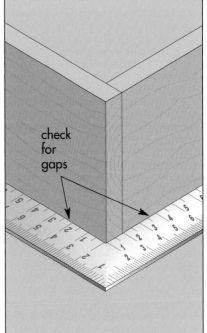

Check with a framing square.
A framing (or carpenter's) square is a convenient double-duty tool for smaller projects. Use it to square up boards and to check measurements. Gaps between the square and the joint can indicate problems.

USING DOWEL AND BISCUIT JOINERY

Professionals and serious woodworking enthusiasts use complicated dovetail and mortise-and-tenon joints. For most projects—including everything in this book—simpler joints will work just as well. Inserting a small piece of wood—a dowel or a biscuit—into two pieces to join them together is a good basic method.

GROOVED DOWELS

Buy ready-made dowels that are fluted, meaning they have grooves running across the lengths that allow space for the glue. To groove solid dowels, drill a hole slightly larger than the dowel in a block of wood and drive an 8d nail into the block so it protrudes $\frac{1}{16}$ inch into the hole. Push the dowel through it several times.

1. Mark for blind dowels.
This method will produce a joint with no visible dowel ends. Dry-fit the pieces with clamps to make sure they will fit snugly. Number the joining pieces so you remember the order of assembly. With the pieces aligned, and clamped if necessary, use a pencil and square to draw a short line spanning the joint for each dowel.

2. Drill holes with a dowel jig.
Choose or make the dowels (see *above*); $\frac{5}{16}$-inch-thick dowels work well for joining 1-by lumber. Be sure to use a guide to drill holes, otherwise the joint will not be straight. For each hole, clamp a dowel jig, aligned with the pencil mark and centered on the thickness of the board. Set the depth gauge, and drill holes slightly more than half the length of the dowels.

3. Glue and clamp.
If you have a number of joints to glue at the same time, be sure to have all the pieces lined up and ready to go before gluing. Squirt glue into all the holes, and tap dowels into the holes on one piece. Assemble, check for square, clamp, and check for square again. Wipe away excess glue with a damp rag, or wait for it to set up a bit and scrape it off.

use bench corner as
a guide for square

dowels

EXPERTS' INSIGHT

WHERE TO USE DOWELS AND BISCUITS

These joints provide great clamping power and rigidity but not much lateral strength. If the dowels or biscuits are stressed along their lengths, they can break. For instance, if two pieces are joined at right angles (*below right*), and downward pressure is put on the horizontal piece, dowels or biscuits will not help.

Don't use dowels or biscuits for a tabletop surface or wherever structural support is needed. However, they work great for door frames and wherever the main concern is to keep joints from pulling apart. Biscuits are easier to install; dowels are stronger.

Dowel reinforcement.
This is simpler than blind doweling, but the dowel ends will show. Clamp the pieces, aligned exactly as you want them to be. (For 45-degree angles, a bench corner can be a guide.) Carefully drill a hole extending through both pieces. The hole does not have to be perfectly straight, but you don't want to poke through a side. Squirt glue onto the dowels, and tap them in with a mallet or a hammer and block of wood. Drive them nearly flush. After the glue dries, sand smooth.

1. Mark and incise for biscuits.
Dry-fit the pieces and position them exactly as you want them. For each biscuit, draw a short line that spans the joint.

Separate the pieces. Set the biscuit joiner to the correct depth for the size biscuit you will use. Align the joiner with the line, and hold the baseplate flat as you cut.

biscuits placed in one edge

2. Glue and clamp the joint.
Dry-fit the boards and biscuits to make sure they can fit tightly. Pull the pieces apart, squirt glue into each incision, and tap in the biscuits. Tap the second board in place, check to see that it is aligned at the ends, and clamp firm. Wipe away excess glue.

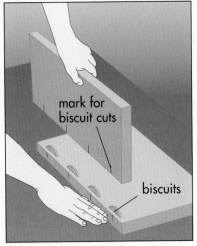

mark for biscuit cuts

biscuits

Assembling at a right angle.
To make sure the biscuits on the vertical piece are at a perfect right angle to the horizontal piece, temporarily clamp another board to it with its top edge flush while you cut the incisions. That makes it easier to hold the baseplate flat.

MAKING DADO, RABBET, AND LAP JOINTS

Often for the sake of appearance and structural integrity, you'll want to build a cabinet or shelf with joints that use old-fashioned joinery, not just fasteners. Here are some handsome joints that, with basic carpentry tools, most novice woodworkers can manage. With a little practice, you'll have a joint that is strong and pleasing to the eye.

A **dado** is a groove that runs across the grain of a board. The depth of a dado is about one-third the thickness of the lumber. For shelves, a dado is usually cut in the shelf standard, and the butt end of a shelf fits into it. A

stopped dado is a variation of the same theme, but the dado ends halfway through the standard—a feature that requires some careful chiseling. The shelf piece is notched to fit into the dado.

The depth of a dado cut is difficult to cut with precision because of imperfections in board faces and saw blades. Whenever possible, cut the dadoes first, then measure for the length of the board that will fit into them.

Rabbets are like dadoes, except that they occur at the end of a board. A rabbet cut forms a ledge that supports the other board. Use rabbet joints when building the

perimeter frame of a project for a stronger and more stable joint than either a butt joint or a miter joint.

Make a **full-lap** joint by cutting a notch as deep as the thickness of the piece to be joined. To make a **half-lap** joint, notch both pieces half their thickness.

The following pages show how to make these joints using a variety of tools. Make sure your tools are sharp to make the work easier and the results better. A table saw is the most efficient tool. With care you can use a router, circular saw, radial arm saw, or a backsaw.

dado

full-lap

stopped dado

rabbet

half-lap

EXPERTS' INSIGHT

CUTTING GROOVES

■ Precise cuts require marking tools that make precise lines. A sharp No. 2 pencil works better than a carpenter's pencil. Scoring with a knife makes the thinnest line and prevents splintering outside the groove.

■ Check the thickness of the board to be inserted into the groove. Some 1-by stock is slightly thicker or thinner than ¾ inch.

■ Cut test grooves on scrap wood before working on the final pieces so you can make minor width or depth adjustments without ruining an expensive piece of wood. Also, the first joints may be less than precise; practice will help.

1. Mark for a dado...
Use a square and a sharp pencil or knife to draw lines indicating the outside edges of a dado or groove. Measure and mark with care. If cutting with a table saw, you don't need to draw lines all the way across, just starter marks. To test for accuracy before cutting, set the board that will be inserted into the groove between the lines.

or for a half-lap.
Set one piece on top of the other, positioned as they will be when the lap joint is completed. Align them carefully and press down firmly. You can then mark the second board the same way. Or, you can mark and cut the notch in the first board, then fit the second piece into the groove and mark it accordingly.

2. Cut with a circular saw...
For a half-lap joint, set the blade depth to half the thickness of the board. For a dado cut, set it to a third of the thickness. Use a speed square or clamped straightedge as a guide. When making each outside cut be careful not to stray outside the line. Make closely spaced cuts in the area to be removed.

or with a backsaw.
Clamp a board to a backsaw for a simple and effective depth guide. Test-cut some grooves to check the depth, and tighten the clamp so the board won't budge as you work. Take care to cut perpendicular to the board; the bottom edge of the depth-guide board will help you test for this.

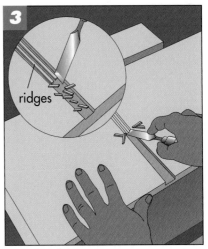

3. Chisel out.
Use a chisel (½ to ¾ inch for dadoes and rabbets, larger for laps) to crack out the ridges. Scrape the surface with the bevel side down to remove large bumps. Finally, turn the chisel bevel-side up and scrape the groove smooth; even small bumps will ruin the joint. At all stages, keep the visible edges clean and straight.

JOINING WITH A TABLE SAW OR ROUTER

A table saw or router can make quick work of cutting long grooves, rabbets, dadoes, and notches for lap joints. However, you will need special equipment: a dado assembly for a table saw and a guide or, better yet, a router table for a router.

You will not have a good view of the cuts being made with either of these tools. The router's body makes it difficult to see the blade, and a table saw cuts a groove beneath the board. Have plenty of scrap pieces on hand so you can test to make sure the grooves will be accurate before starting.

YOU'LL NEED

TIME: Setting up may take 5 to 10 minutes. Sawing takes less than a minute per cut.
SKILLS: Measuring and marking; use of the tool.
TOOLS: Table saw, router, dado assembly, router guide or table.

Table saw dado assembly.
With two outside cutters and four or more ⅛-inch chippers, you can make precise grooves of various thicknesses. You may need a throat plate with an extra-wide opening to accommodate the assembly; test by turning the blades by hand to make sure they do not scrape. A less precise alternative is an adjustable dado blade that wobbles to make a wide cut.

Crosscut the dado.
Unplug the saw and install a dado blade and wide throat plate. Make test cuts on a scrap piece to set the depth. Make sure the miter guide is square, and use the rip fence with a clamped board to measure for the location of the dado (see page 29). For long boards, attach a facing strip to the miter gauge. For stopped dadoes (page 38), clamp a stop block to the table.

Cutting a long groove.
Install the dado assembly and clamp the rip fence so it is parallel to the blade. Clamp one or two featherboards to protect against kickback. Test on scrap pieces until the cuts are correctly positioned and at the proper depth. **Caution:** The blade is not visible sometimes. Keep your hands well away from the blade. Use a push stick (page 41) when ending a cut.

Rabbet with a standard blade.

Adjust for the depth of the rabbet and test on a scrap piece. Attach a piece of wood to the side of the rip fence, and adjust it so the saw cuts on the waste side of the cut line. Clamp a featherboard to the fence and run the piece through.

Remove the featherboard and make the second cut by holding the piece vertically against the fence. Test your setup on scrap pieces and make adjustments as needed. (With rabbets as deep as they are wide, you won't need to adjust the blade or the fence.)

Rabbet with a dado blade.

Unplug the saw and install the dado-cutting assembly. Slide the rip fence nearly against the blades and clamp a featherboard onto the fence. Test-cut scraps until you have the correct depth and width, then cut the real thing.

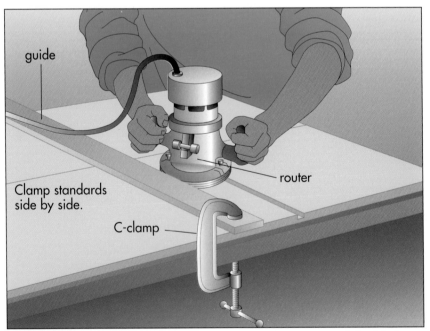

Dadoes with a router.

A router with a straight bit quickly cuts a groove. Make sure the guides are tightly clamped, and firmly press the tool against the guide as you cut; a moment's lapse can make a crooked groove. Always push or pull the router against the rotation of the blade—the direction of most resistance. If you move with the rotation of the blade, the router will probably skate away. Hone your techniques on scraps. For grooves that line up, clamp the standards together.

MAKING A CABINET DOOR

There are two basic types of cabinet door: A *panel* door is more complicated to make and requires a table saw; a *slab* door is a single piece of wood, usually plywood. Slab doors are usually edged with trim for a neater appearance and to prevent warping. In addition to selecting a door style, decide how the door will fit in the cabinet (see page 44). A *flush* door fits inside the cabinet frame and must be sized so there is an even ⅛-inch gap all around. An *inset* door has a rabbeted edge around its perimeter that covers the frame. An *overlay* door fits entirely over the frame and is the easiest to make.

YOU'LL NEED

TIME: 2 hours for a panel door; or a half hour for a trimmed slab.
SKILLS: Measuring and cutting.
TOOLS: Table saw, power or hand miter saw, drill.

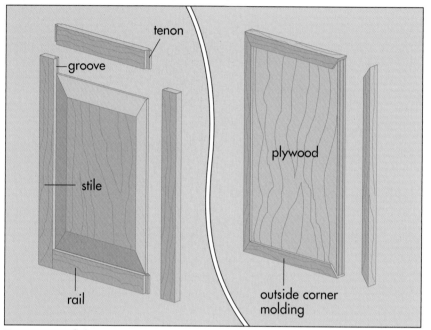

Two types of door.
A panel door has two horizontal *rails* and two vertical *stiles*. All four pieces have a groove into which the *panel* fits. Each rail has a tenon on each end that fits into the groove of the rail just as the panel does. The panel could be a flat piece of thin plywood, but a more attractive option is to bevel the edges of a wide 1-by board.

The slab door shown has been trimmed simply, using outside corner molding on the perimeter. A simple measure like this dresses up a door.

1. Bevel-cut the panel.
If the panel will be wider than 11½ inches (the width of a 1×12), clamp and glue pieces edge-to-edge (see page 34). Fasten a 1×6 or 1×8 to the rip fence to keep the workpiece from wobbling while you work. Adjust the blade so the bottom edge of the bevel will be just thick enough to fit into the groove you will make in the rails (see step 3 on page 43). To give the panel a "step," adjust so the top edge of the cut will be ⅛ inch below the face of the board. If you don't want a step, raise the blade to cut all the way through. Remove the blade guard, and keep your hands well away from the blade. Bevel-cut all four edges.

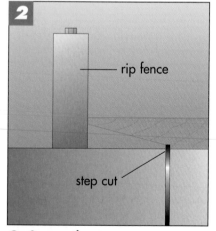

2. Square the step.
If you chose to have a stepped bevel, square the blade and adjust it down so it cuts only ⅛ inch deep. Align the fence so that the blade will cut just the top edge of the bevel and square it up. Test with scraps; this calls for precise adjustment. Run all four sides of the panel through the saw.

3. Groove the rails and stiles.

Install a dado assembly (see page 40) so it cuts the same width as the thickness of the door panel at the perimeter. Test cut on a scrap and to make sure the panel will fit the groove snugly. With the 1×6 or 1×8 clamped to the fence, adjust the fence so the blade will cut in the exact center of a board edge. (Test for this by cutting a groove, turning the piece around, and cutting again.) Cut a groove on the inside edge of all rails and stiles.

4. Cut tenons.

Each rail must have a tenon on both ends. A tenon should be ½ inch long and as thick as the door panel. This means that the rail itself should be 1 inch longer than the distance between stiles.

Set a dado assembly to cut half the board's thickness, minus the thickness of the tenon. Attach a straight piece of 1-by to the miter guide so you can hold the rail firmly as you cut. Clamp a scrap piece to the front end of the rip fence to use as a spacing guide (see page 29). Adjust the fence so that it positions the rail to cut a ½-inch-wide tenon. Cut one side of the tenon, flip the board over, and cut the other.

Experiment on scrap pieces to achieve the precise blade height and the exact width adjustment so that the tenon fits snugly into a stile groove. Take your time, test your setup, and get it right: This is the step that appearances are determined.

5. Clamp and glue.

Sand any saw marks on the panel. Dry-fit the pieces to make sure they fit tightly. Remove the stiles and apply glue to the rail tenons. (Don't glue the panel into the groove; it must be allowed to expand and contract with changes in humidity without stressing the stiles and rail.) Clamp and let dry.

Achieve a raised look.

You can dress up a new or old slab door by installing moldings. Two bands of molding, running either vertically or horizontally, add elegance to any slab door. Or miter-cut four pieces of thin molding, such as fluted screen bead, to form a frame on the door. Even chair rail can be applied for an ornamental look.

Plan all the doors at the same time: Horizontal pieces should all be at the same height, and the distance between molding and door edge should be the same for all doors.

INSTALLING HINGED DOORS

Most cabinet projects call for unobtrusive hinges that, if visible at all, meld with any decor. Of the types commonly available, Euro-style hinges (see page 46) are the most expensive and are entirely concealed. **Overlay** and **offset** hinges (*right*) are mostly hidden, with only the smaller hinge leaf visible. If you have flush doors, a **concealed wraparound** hinge (*right*) will be nearly invisible. (For hinges designed to be displayed, see page 19.)

When building new cabinets, install hinges and knobs last, after the doors and drawers are painted or finished. If you want to dress up old cabinets by painting or refinishing, remove the hinges and knobs first. (It is nearly impossible to paint around hinges, and removing them takes surprisingly little time.)

A neat installation of smoothly functioning hinges requires care and patience. All the hinges in a row of cabinets should be at the same height. If a change of height is required, the change should be consistent. Also, cabinet hinges determine the height and angle of doors. If a hinge is installed even $\frac{1}{16}$ inch out of alignment, the door will be noticeably out of line with the other doors. If the hinges are not adjustable—and most, except Euro-style hinges, are not—it will be difficult to move one slightly. Work systematically with attention to detail.

You will find yourself often alternating between drilling pilot holes and driving screws. Have two drills on hand, one with a pilot bit and one equipped with a magnetic sleeve and screwdriver bit. Cordless drills make this work much easier. Most hinge screws call for a No. 1 phillips bit; using the more common but too-large No. 2 bit will be frustrating.

offset

overlay

concealed wraparound

Mark with an awl

Installing an overlay hinge.
With the door face down, place the hinges about 2 inches from the top and bottom; use a spacer or jig to ensure that all the hinges in a group of cabinets are placed in identical positions. Drill pilot holes in the exact center of each hole, and drive the screws that come with the hinges.

Next, position the door on the cabinet exactly as it will be when hung; using spacers or clamp-on guides. Have a helper hold it while you work. Mark for the pilot holes using an awl, then remove the door to drill the pilot holes. If you feel confident that the door is firmly and correctly in place, drill the pilot holes through the hinge holes and drive the screws in the same operation.

EXPERTS' INSIGHT

ALWAYS DRILL PILOT HOLES

Constantly alternating between drilling pilot holes and driving screws may seem tedious, and you will be tempted to skip an occasional pilot hole and just drive in the screw. Resist that temptation. Though a hinge screw is small, it can easily crack a cabinet stile. A cracked stile must be glued and clamped, a time-consuming process. Also, pilot holes make it much easier to drive the screws straight; screws driven at an angle tend to look unprofessional.

1. Measure for an inset door.
An inset or "lipped" door is ¼ inch larger on all sides than the opening. The rabbet running all around the door is ⅜ inch wide, giving a clearance of ⅛ inch between the inside of the rabbet and the cabinet. You must measure carefully to get a good fit.

2. Install an offset hinge.
Place the door face down, and install the hinges about 2 inches from the top and bottom. Use the same spacing for all the doors.

The key is to center the inset door in the opening. Place ⅛-inch hardboard spacers on the bottom and one side of the opening. Set the door on the spacers (carefully, since you won't be able to see the spacers). Align the door precisely; you may have to pull it away from a spacer slightly. Mark for pilot holes with an awl, or drill pilot holes through the hinge holes, and then drive screws.

Install a butt or concealed wraparound hinge.
For flush doors, measure an equal distance from top and bottom, as for a concealed wraparound hinge (see page 44). Install a wraparound hinge on the door.

For a butt hinge, use a chisel and knife to cut a mortise, and install one leaf of the hinge in the mortise. Use two finish nails as spacers, and center the door in the opening so that there is a consistent ⅛-inch gap all around. Use a sharp pencil to mark the top and bottom of the hinge. Remove the door, and cut a mortise as thick as the hinge leaf. Position the hinges, mark and drill pilot holes, then drive the screws.

TOOLS TO USE

USE A JIG TO MARK FOR HINGES AND PULLS
Using a tape measure to mark the position for each hinge is not only time-consuming, but could cause inaccuracies. To ensure uniformity, develop a method for spacing all hinges and pulls the same distance from door and drawer face edges and follow it consistently. Here are two ways to do that:

■ Use a small piece of wood as a jig. Hold it against the door edge, press the hinge up against it, and mark for pilot holes.

■ Or use another hinge. It is standard practice to install hinges one hinge length from the door edge. Just hold one hinge against the door edge, slide the other up against it, and mark for pilot holes.

1. To install a concealed hinge, drill a recess hole.

Cut the recess hole with a Forstner bit (*below*), or make a template and cut it with a router. The hole in the template should be the diameter of the recess hole, plus the thickness of the router's bushing (see page 31).

2. Mark the stile.

Insert the hinge in the door, drill pilot holes, and drive the screws. Position the door against the face frame. While a helper holds it in the correct position, mark the location of the hinges on the stile.

3. Install and adjust.

With the door open, have the helper hold the hinges against the marks on the stile. Carefully try the movement of the door until it fits smoothly. Center the adjusting screws in the slots provided. Loosen or tighten the screws to adjust the position of the door.

Euro-style hinge.

This type of hinge can be used for an overlay or flush door. It is the easiest hinge to adjust, allowing you to move it up and down, in and out. One side fits into a recess hole in the door, which you can drill with a Forstner bit or cut with a router. The arm slides onto a mounting bracket. To install it, first mount the hinge in the recess hole. Install the mounting bracket onto the inside of the cabinet, then slide the hinge arm onto the mounting bracket.

Glass-door hinge.

Glass doors are always flush, fitting inside the cabinet. To mount the type shown, drill a pair of holes (usually ¼-inch) near the edge of the top rail and another pair near the edge of the bottom rail. Tap a sleeve into the hole nearest the end, and a catch into the other hole. Slip hinges into the sleeves, fit the glass door into the hinges, adjust the door so it fits inside the opening, and tighten the holding screws on the hinges.

INSTALLING CATCHES AND PULLS

Fastening cabinet catches calls for no special skills, but you must have patience. You will often be working in tight places, and you might not have enough room to drill and drive screws straight.

Position a catch as close as possible to the handle or pull to reduce stress to the hinges. In most cases, the catch is mounted to the cabinet and the strike to the door. Usually, you should mount base-cabinet pulls and catches near the top of the door and wall-cabinet pulls and catches near the bottom of the door. A magnetic screwdriver or a magnetic sleeve holds the screw on the bit, speeding the job.

YOU'LL NEED

TIME: About 15 minutes for an average catch.
SKILLS: Drilling pilot holes and driving screws; measuring.
TOOLS: Drill, screwdriver.

Install catches.
To mount any kind of catch, attach the catch first, then the strike. Drill pilot holes to avoid splintering wood and to ensure that the screws go in straight.

Whenever possible, use the catch itself to help with marking.

For a spring catch like the one shown *above,* attach the catch and insert the strike into it. Close the door firmly. The marking points on the front of the strike will make indentations in the door showing you where to mount the strike.

Use a template to drill for door pulls.
All the door pulls in a group of cabinets should be at the same height or else the cabinets will look unprofessional. It is easy to achieve this uniformity if you use a template like the one shown. Drill holes in a piece of wood spaced where you want them on each door. Hold the template with its edges flush with the door edges, then drill the holes.

Install a decorative latch.
These latches usually work for flush doors only. Installing them is simple. With the door closed, position the latch with its edge flush with the edge of the door, drill pilot holes, and drive screws. Close the door and place the strike on the cabinet so that the latch can close on it. Drill pilot holes and drive screws to install the strike.

INSTALLING SLIDING DOORS

Purchase metal tracks made for sliding doors made of ¾-inch plywood. The top track has deeper channels; the other track goes on the bottom. If the cabinet is faced with a frame, fit the tracks against the back side of the frame. If not, position them about ¼ inch in from the front edge of the cabinet.

Protruding door pulls would get in the way as one door slides past the other. Instead, drill holes for pulls. Position the holes about ¾ inch from the outside edge of each door, centered vertically. Drill through with a hole saw, and sand the edges. Or drill partway through with a Forstner bit and tap in a round metal door pull.

Fit the door panels—the rear one first—by lifting them up into the top track and dropping them into the bottom track.

hole saw

Upper track is deeper.

Lower track has shallow guides.

BUILDING AND INSTALLING A DRAWER

For drawers no larger than 24 inches square, use ⅜-inch or ½-inch plywood for the sides and bottom. Usually the face piece is made of ¾-inch stock to match the thickness of doors.

Manufactured drawers often use complicated dovetail joints, but the rabbet-and-groove joints shown are easier to construct and are strong enough.

Make drawers at least 2 inches shorter than the depth of the cabinet and ¼ inch narrower than the width of the opening (not including the face piece).

1

face piece

⅜"×¾" rabbets

1" screw

¼" plywood

¾" plywood

YOU'LL NEED

TIME: A couple of hours to make one drawer.
SKILLS: Cutting grooves, rabbets; fastening nails, screws.
TOOLS: Power saw, drill, tape measure, framing square.

1. Cut the parts.
Cut the back and front pieces to ¾ inch less than the total width of the drawer; cut the side pieces to the total length. Use a table saw, radial arm saw, or circular saw to cut grooves in the sides and front, ¼ inch up from the bottom. Cut ⅜-inch-deep by ¾-inch-wide rabbets in both ends of the side pieces. Cut the face piece larger than the front. Assemble the pieces and measure for a bottom that fits in the grooves.

2. Assemble the parts.

Align the face piece and attach it with four 1-inch general-purpose screws through the front piece and into the face piece. Rip-cut the back piece so its top is flush with the top of the side pieces when it sits on the bottom piece. Squeeze glue onto the rabbets and the ends of the front and back pieces, and assemble the four outside pieces. Slide the bottom in; do not apply glue to the grooves. Check for square, and drive 3d finish nails through the rabbet joints, and up through the bottom and into the back piece.

3. Choose drawer glides.

Side-mount drawer glides, which are more expensive than center-mount drawer glides with side rollers, operate more smoothly, last longer, and can handle heavier loads. Inexpensive models use plastic rollers, better-quality side-mounts feature ball-bearing rollers. They are available in lengths from 12 to 28 inches. Choose glides that are an inch or so shorter than the length of the drawer.

EXPERTS' INSIGHT

DRAWER TIPS

■ Every drawer must be square. If it's out of square, the face will not rest flush against the cabinet front, and the drawer may rub against the cabinet sides.

■ Do not attach the drawer bottom with glue or nails anywhere except at the rear piece. Otherwise, it will put stress on the rabbet joints when it expands and contracts due to changes in humidity.

■ Keep the drawer dry. Tossing in wet silverware, for instance, can eventually cause warping. For protection, line the bottom of the drawer with shelf paper.

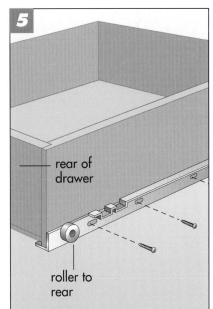

4. Attach slide to cabinet.

You may need to install a nailer so you'll have something to attach the slide to. Drill pilot holes and drive screws to attach the glides so they are level, the front edges flush with the front of the cabinet.

5. Attach to drawer.

Install the other pieces of the glide to the sides of the drawer. The rollers go to the rear. Slip the rollers into the cabinet-mounted glide pieces, and test for smooth operation.

EDGING AND FINISHING

Once you've finished building a project, you can complete the finishing touches—edging, filling holes, sanding, and staining or painting. The square corners and tight joints will not be noticed if the wood surface looks unfinished. Conversely, an imperfectly constructed cabinet becomes respectable with careful sanding and staining.

Tools for finishing are simple: a putty knife, a sanding block (or an electric sander if you are doing a lot of work), a paintbrush, and a small pile of rags may be all you need.

Remove all visible glue before finishing. Either wipe excess glue with a damp rag while it is wet or wait for it to partially harden and then scrape most of it away with a putty knife. After you have used one of these methods, wait until the residual glue is completely dry, then sand it away completely.

Edging and tape.
Plywood edges are unattractive. Most edges are covered during the course of building shelves and cabinets, but often some remain exposed. It's easier to cover an edge than to finish or paint it.

Shelf edge and screen mold are ¾ inch wide and about ¼ inch thick. If you install them with finish nails, you will have nail heads to set and fill, and you may crack the molding. Instead, apply glue and then tape the molding tight until the glue sets.

Or, purchase iron-on veneer tape. Use scissors to cut a piece a bit longer than needed. Press it in place with a hot iron until the glue melts. Wait a couple of minutes, then trim the waste with a knife and sand the edges lightly.

Filling holes.
Use colored wood filler after staining, or use stainable putty before staining. Push the filler into holes with your finger, then scrape with a putty knife. Either wipe away the excess with a damp rag or allow the putty to dry and then sand it smooth.

Sanding.
Attach sandpaper to a sanding block rather than using a loose piece of sandpaper. Sand with medium pressure—don't force it—and move in the direction of the grain. Examine your work from various angles and feel the surface.

TOOLS TO USE

POWER SANDERS

Power sanders are helpful for large jobs, although hand-sanding is often nearly as fast. If you have gouges in the wood and need to remove 1/16 inch or so of surface, a power sander is better. Here are the options:

■ A *belt sander* takes away wood fiber quickly: Be careful: One careless move and you could gouge the wood. So use a belt sander only for heavy sanding or for shaping.

■ Standard *vibrating sanders* and many "detail sanders" are much safer, but you may find they remove wood more slowly than hand-sanding.

■ A *random-orbit sander* is often the best choice because it removes wood fairly quickly with minimal risk of gouging the board.

lint-free rag

Apply stain.
Choose a penetrating stain and experiment with scrap pieces of the same species before staining your project. Apply heavily with a brush, wait a few minutes, then wipe with a lint-free rag (not a paper towel). Make it darker by applying and wiping stain again; lighten by rubbing with a cloth moistened with water or thinner. After staining, apply a clear finish (see chart, *below*).

EXPERTS' INSIGHT

PAINTING TECHNIQUES

Painting requires more care than many people realize. Don't just cover the board with color; aim for a uniform texture of brush strokes or roller texture. Here are some tips:

■ Don't expect paint to cover imperfections such as pronounced grain, bumps, or holes. Often, paint will actually accentuate these imperfections.

■ To brush on paint, first use short strokes running across the grain. Then use long strokes with the grain. Finish with light, long strokes, moving in one direction, not back and forth.

■ Consider using a roller. It produces a bumpy "stipple," which you may find more attractive than brush strokes.

CHOOSING AND APPLYING CLEAR FINISHES

Type	Characteristics and Application Tips
Oil Polyurethane	Hard and long-lasting, but tends to yellow with time; yellowing will not be noticeable if it is applied over a stain. Apply with a bristle brush.
Water-Based Polyurethane	Not as durable as oil-based, but it doesn't yellow. Apply with a synthetic brush.
Oil Finishes	Not as durable as polyurethane, but many prefer its appearance, and it is easier to repair. Apply several coats. "Danish" oil, which is available mixed with stain, is the easiest to apply.
Varnish	An older product that has oils and resins. "Spar" varnish stays flexible and is suitable for outdoor use. Apply with a bristle brush.
Shellac	An alcohol-based product that is thick and dries quickly. Easily marred by water or alcohol. Apply with a bristle brush.
Lacquer	Used mostly by professionals, lacquer produces a silky surface but is difficult to use. Apply many coats with an ox-hair brush.

cherry

walnut

natural

painted

Several types of finishes.
Both matte and glossy clear finishes subtly alter the look of stained wood. Use semigloss or gloss paints for easy cleaning.

LIGHTING FOR CABINETS

Many a gloomy kitchen can be brightened with cabinet lighting. This added illumination can make food preparation more enjoyable and make a small room seem larger. Place under-cabinet and cove lights so they will be out of sight; they should illuminate, not glare. Low-voltage halogen lights are the easiest to install if cabinets are already in place. If adding new cabinets, consider running cables and installing fluorescent lights.

YOU'LL NEED

TIME: A couple of hours for a set of halogens; running cable for fluorescent lights takes longer.
SKILLS: Basic wiring.
TOOLS: Drill, lineman's pliers, keyhole or reciprocating saw, screwdriver.

transformer

halogen light
with lens

power box

halogen
light base

remote switch
receiver

1. Plan for a halogen system.
Map out the job, and purchase a set of halogen under-cabinet lights with all the lights and wire you need. These lights get very hot, so place them away from combustible materials and out of the reach of children. Drill inconspicuous holes and run the thin wire into the cabinet. Install the power box and transformer out of sight. Run the power cord from a receptacle to the transformer. Coil any excess wire and tuck it out of the way.

base

reflector ring

halogen bulb

lens cover

2. Install the lights.
Disassemble a light, and attach the fixture base to the underside of the cabinet with short screws; make sure they do not poke through the wood into the cabinet interior. Connect the wires in the light, and staple down running wire. Install the reflector ring, and plug in the bulb. Install the lens cover.

battery

switch base

cover plate

3. Connect the switch.
The switch operates by battery and is mounted flush to the wall, so you can easily place it anywhere on a wall or cabinet. Screw the housing to the wall by driving screws into a stud. Or drill holes in the wall surface, tap in plastic anchors, and drive screws into the anchors. Attach the cover plate to the housing.

1. Run cable for fluorescent lights.

Hire an electrician if you do not know how to run power from a box. With the cabinets removed, mark the walls carefully to show where the cables will emerge from the wall. (Disassemble the lights to find out exactly where the cable will enter them.) Plan to pull the cables through the lower rear lip of the cabinet if it has one, or just below the bottom of the cabinet.

Run power to the switch, then to the first light; run a cable out of the first light to the second and so, on until you come to the last light. To run the cable past studs, cut holes in the wallboard or plaster and make notches with a reciprocating saw. These holes will be covered by the cabinets.

If the cabinets have lower lips, drill holes or cut notches for the cable. Install the cabinets.

2. Connect the lights.

For each light, punch out the knockout and install a cable clamp. Run the cable into the fixture, and screw the fixture to the cabinet. Strip and connect wires. Attach the cover plate and install a fluorescent bulb. Turn on the power and test. If the light is glaring at eye level, install a strip of wood in front to deflect the glare downward.

Cove Lighting.

Subtle light from the top of a cabinet gently illuminates the room. Set fluorescent fixtures on top of your cabinets, and make sure they are not visible to people standing in the room. (Because the electrical lines and fixtures are hidden from view, you are not as restricted with the installation.) You may want to add cove molding on top of the cabinets to help hide the lights.

Run electrical cable from a switch to the area above the cabinets. Hook up the lights. Usually, you can let them sit on top of the cabinet.

EXPERTS' INSIGHT

LIGHTING A KITCHEN

Most well-lighted kitchens have these types of lights:

■ Overhead and/or cove lighting provides general illumination for the whole room. A kitchen should have at least 300 watts of incandescent lighting.

■ Under-cabinet lights are essential because a person's body comes between overhead lights and a countertop. Plan for one 20-watt fluorescent light or one 12-watt halogen light for every 3 feet of running countertop space.

■ Install accent lights for special areas. Direct some track lights toward the sink, or hang a light above a dining area.

INSTALLING WALL-MOUNTED OPEN SHELVING

These are simple to install if you are careful to plumb and level the standards. Attach brackets or standards with screws driven deeply into studs, or they may pull out of the the wall when loaded.

Use enough supports so the boards do not sag over time; see the chart on page 57. If you plan to put very heavy objects on the shelves, add more supports so the shelf won't sag. For a stronger shelf that can span farther, reinforce the front and back edges with 1×2 attached to the underside of the shelf between the brackets.

YOU'LL NEED

TIME: A couple of hours to install a simple set of shelves.
SKILLS: Measuring, leveling, driving screws.
TOOLS: Drill, level, tape measure.

1. Find studs.
To find the location of a stud, tap on the wall and listen for a less-hollow sound. Or drill a series of test holes in a place where they will be covered. Better yet, use a stud sensor.

2. Secure first standard.
Place a standard over a stud at the desired height. Stamped numerals tell you it is right-side up. Drive a screw through the topmost hole at least 1½ inches into a stud. Check for level, and drive more screws.

3. Add other standards.
Use a level, or a level set on a long straight board, to find the correct height for the standard on the other end of the shelf system. Lightly draw a horizontal line near the intersecting vertical line marking the nearest stud.

Position a standard right-side up, with its top edge at the intersection of the two lines. Drive a screw, check for plumb, and drive more screws.

If you will have standards in between the two standards on the ends, use a straightedge set on top of the outside standards to mark for their height. Check them for plumb, and attach them with screws.

4. Hang the shelves.
Use brackets that are the right length for the width of your shelf. Slip each into two slots and push down until it is secure. Count slots to make sure all the brackets for a shelf are level. When they are installed, simply set the shelf on top. Because the shelves are open-ended, you may need bookends.

1. To install a wall-mounted bracket, secure the first bracket.
Locate a stud, determine the height of the shelf, and position the bracket. Drive a screw through a hole and into the stud, but do not tighten it completely. Use a level to plumb the bracket (a small torpedo level is handy for this), then drive the other screw and tighten the first screw.

2. Locate other bracket.
Set a level on top of the first bracket and use it to find the height for the bracket near the other end of the shelf. It should be attached to a stud as well. Plumb the bracket and attach it with screws. If there are intermediate brackets, use a straightedge laid on top of the outside brackets to determine their height.

3. Attach shelf (and covers).
Lay a shelf on top of the brackets. If the wall is not straight, you may want to trim the shelf so it fits tightly against the wall. Attach the shelf to the brackets by drilling pilot holes and driving ⅝-inch screws up through the bracket. The bracket shown has a decorative cover; simply snap it into place.

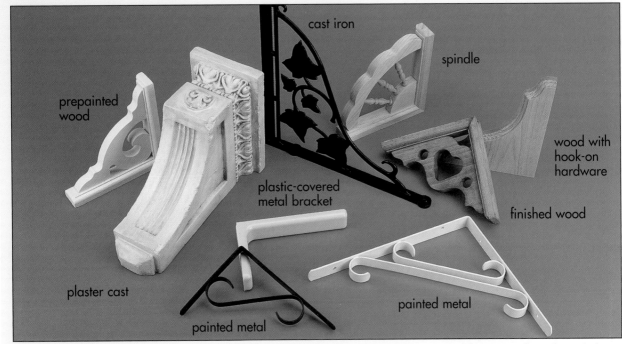

Bracket options.
Choose from a variety of decorative and utility brackets. Diagonal supports lend extra strength but may get in the way of a lower shelf. Choose a bracket nearly as long as the width of your shelf. For the greatest strength, place the long arm on the wall and the short arm under the shelf.

Brackets are often designed to hide the fasteners; some hook onto screws partially driven into a wood standard so that no hardware is visible.

USING OTHER BRACKET OPTIONS

Hardware stores and home centers have a host of options for shelf supports. In addition to the ones we've shown, consider using coated-wire shelving in places other than a closet (see pages 98–99).

A renovation supply store or an architectural salvage yard carry a variety of interesting old brackets. You may need to strip and/or paint them, but the results will be well worth your effort.

You can make your own designs and modifications. Design your own wood bracket (see the template *below*). Trim the shelf out with moldings of your choice.

A shelf-support system not only must provide a strong bracket to withstand downward pressure, but it also must ensure that the bracket and shelf do not pull away from the wall. Simply screwing the bracket to the wall may not be sufficient; use a strip attached to the wall, as in the design *at right*.

1. For a decorative shelf, cut the shelf and add edging.
Cut a piece of ¾-inch plywood or a 1-by board to the desired dimensions. For edging, choose a ¾-inch-wide screen bead, and miter-cut three pieces. Attach the edging using tape and glue (see pages 30 and 50).

Cut a 1×3 cleat to support the back of the shelf and to allow you to attach the brackets anywhere on the wall, since they do not need to be directly screwed into studs. Cut the cleat the width of the shelf, minus the thickness of the brackets and the desired overhangs.

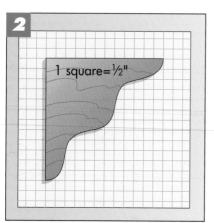

2. Design a bracket.
The bracket should be about an inch shorter than the depth of the shelf. Take the design shown *above* to a copy center, and enlarge it until it fits the bracket.

Or draw your own design on graph paper. Use a compass to make a series of connecting arcs. The wider the bracket is in the middle, the stronger it will be.

3. Cut the bracket.
Cut out the design and trace it onto a piece of 2-by lumber so the bracket's grain will be horizontal when installed.

Clamp the board onto a table corner so that the area under the cut is clear. Cut the line with a saber saw (see page 27). Use the first bracket as a template to mark for the second. Sand the edges.

4. Install the shelf.
Position the cleat level on the wall, and mark the location of studs. Drill pilot holes and drive pairs of screws at least 2 inches into each stud. To attach the brackets to the cleat, drill pilot holes and drive two 1½-inch screws. Counterbore and plug the screw holes (see page 33). Attach the shelf to the cleat and brackets with 4d finish nails.

Slide-in utility shelves.

This system allows you to move shelves by sliding them out and in again. It produces useful utility shelves but may be too rough-looking for living rooms.

Clamp 2×4 standards, four for each shelf, side by side, and cut ¾-inch square dadoes every 2 or 3 inches (see pages 38–41). Strengthen outside standards by screwing them to other 2×4s; screw two dadoed 2×4s together to make inside standards.

MEASUREMENTS

HOW MANY SUPPORTS DO YOU NEED?

For shelves that will be loaded with books, space brackets close enough to each other to prevent the shelf from sagging.

Size of Board	Bracket Spacing
¾-inch plywood	32"
1×6 or 1×8	18"
1×10 or 1×12	24"
¾-inch particleboard	18"
2×10 or 2×12	36"
½-inch acrylic	18"
⅜-inch glass	16"

1. To dress up metal standards, cut a groove in hardwood.

Cut a groove the width and depth of the shelf standard into a piece of 1×2 hardwood (see pages 38–41). This is easy with a table saw or router attached to a table. To groove-cut a piece this thin with a circular saw, clamp it firmly to a wider 1-by piece to provide a flat surface for the saw's baseplate.

2. Install the standard.

Clean out the groove with a chisel, sand, and stain or paint if desired. At least apply a clear finish, or the wood will become dingy and difficult to clean.

Cut the 1×2 to the exact length of the standard. Slip the standard into the groove. Drill pilot holes the same thickness as the mounting screws in all the holes.

3. Attach to wall.

Position the standard at a stud, right-side up, at the correct height, and use a level to check for plumb (see page 54). Drive screws through the holes in the standard. Choose the length of the screws carefully; they need to go at least 1½ inches into a wall stud. Install supports and mounted shelves.

MOUNTING BRACKETLESS SHELVES

Because these shelves have no visible means of support, they seem to float on the wall. They are well-supported, however. Lengths of steel reinforcing bar (the "rebar" used to strengthen concrete) penetrate deep into wall studs and into the shelves.

Determine the spacing precisely—it will be difficult to adjust these shelves later. Once you have drawn level lines on the wall, stand back and make sure they look parallel to the floor. If your floor is obviously out of level, you may want to compensate somewhat with the lines. To make the installation easier, use a drill guide so the holes in the shelves and wall are perfectly straight.

YOU'LL NEED
TIME: Half a day to lay out and install six shelves.
SKILLS: Careful measuring, leveling, and drilling.
TOOLS: Drill with guide, level, tape measure, saw, hacksaw.

1. Lay out on the wall.
On graph paper, diagram the shelves. Choose either a regular pattern or random placement.

Use a stud sensor to locate studs; mark with pieces of tape that can be pulled off without marring the wall. Use a level to draw horizontal lines indicating the centers of the shelves' edges.

Now find the exact center of the studs by drilling exploratory holes or driving a nail at several points. (Make sure that these holes will be covered by the shelf.) At every stud, draw an **X** to indicate the center of the shelf and the center of the stud.

2. Drill holes.
At each **X**, drill a starter hole with an awl or a nail so the drill bit cannot skate away. Using a drill guide to ensure that the holes will be level and straight, drill ⅜-inch holes 3¼ inches deep to accept the lengths of rebar.

3. Mark shelf edge.
With a hacksaw, cut pieces of rebar to 3 inches plus the width of the shelf, less 2 inches. Tap a piece of rebar into each hole. With a helper, hold the shelf flat against the wall, underneath the rebar pieces. Mark the location of each piece of rebar on the shelf edge.

4. Install shelf.
Use the drill with a guide to bore ⅜-inch holes in the center of the shelf edge for each piece of rebar. Drill carefully, and make the holes an inch or so shallower than the board width. Fit the rods into the holes, and tap the shelf flush against the wall.

MAKING SHELVES OF FOUND OBJECTS

These ideas harken back to the creative shelving solutions found in dorm rooms and first apartments—still a classic for informal living areas. If a low-budget, quick shelf suits your plans, consider these options for a basement family room, a home office, or a children's play room. However, if you have children in your household, limit stacked shelves to no more than 3 feet—any higher and they might topple if climbed on. Let these designs spur your imagination to put other found objects to use.

YOU'LL NEED

TIME: Gathering the materials will take the most time.
SKILLS: Sawing.
TOOLS: Drill, saber saw, or handsaw, depending on the project.

wine crate

Wine crates.
These often can be purchased for a few dollars each at a wine store; sometimes they are given away. Stack the crates randomly. Lay one horizontally for tall books. Use one vertically, with a ⅜-inch piece of plywood nailed across the middle to form two shelves for shorter books. For stability, anchor some of the boxes to the wall by driving screws into studs.

2×8 or 2×10

flue pipe

Chimney flue pipes and board.
Purchase round clay flue pipe for the vertical supports. With a saber saw, cut the ends of 2×8s or 2×10s in half-circles, to mirror the curve of the pipes. Sand the rough edges. Stain or paint the shelves; the flue pipe is porous enough to take stain. Test the stain on a scrap piece of pipe first.

1×10

old encyclopedias

Books and boards.
Old encyclopedias fastened together make handsome shelf standards. Clamp each stack and bore two ¼-inch holes down through it. Countersink the holes with a ½-inch bit and slip in a threaded shaft cut slightly shorter than the stack is high. Attach washers and nuts and seal the stacks with clear polyurethane.

BUILDING A FIXED-SHELF UNIT

Whether you need a freestanding or wall-mounted shelf, a basic box with fixed shelves is sturdy and can be adapted to most any style. Freestanding units can be stacked and moved into new and different configurations; several wall-mounted units can be combined for ease of installation.

Beginner carpenters can make this unit. Butt-joining the outside corners produces a clean-looking joint with little trouble. If you have some carpentry experience, you may want the cleaner look of mitered joints. Try mitered joints only if you are sure of your ability to make perfectly straight miter cuts; gaps will ruin the project.

To support the shelves, simple butt joints can be strong and stable if fastened with screws. Or reinforce a butt joint by attaching a cleat under the shelf.

A dado joint is the strongest and virtually guarantees that the shelves and the outside pieces will not warp. When you get the hang of dadoes, cutting them is not time-consuming.

The shelves are simple and require precise cutting. Before starting, test your power saw with scrap pieces to make sure you can cut perfectly straight and square without raising splinters. Use a sharp blade. Often it is possible to stack pieces roughly cut to length and make the final cuts on several shelves at once.

The miter-jointed box shown in the steps on page 61 is the most difficult method.

YOU'LL NEED

TIME: Most of a day to build a fixed unit with several shelves and a back.
SKILLS: Accurate measuring and cutting, drilling and driving screws, cutting dadoes.
TOOLS: Power saw, drill, hammer, tape measure, chisel.

EXPERTS' INSIGHT

FINISHING OR PAINTING A SHELF UNIT

■ Painting a cabinet can be very time-consuming, especially if you need to brush on two coats. Painting boards before they are put together is much easier and faster. Give the boards a primer coat before assembly. (Many primers dry in an hour or less.) If you want two coats of paint over the primer, apply one coat before assembly.

■ If you need to paint a number of units, consider buying an inexpensive paint sprayer or renting an airless sprayer.

■ Staining assembled shelves is difficult; it's hard to get a consistent color in the corners. Stain the pieces, assemble them, and then apply a finish.

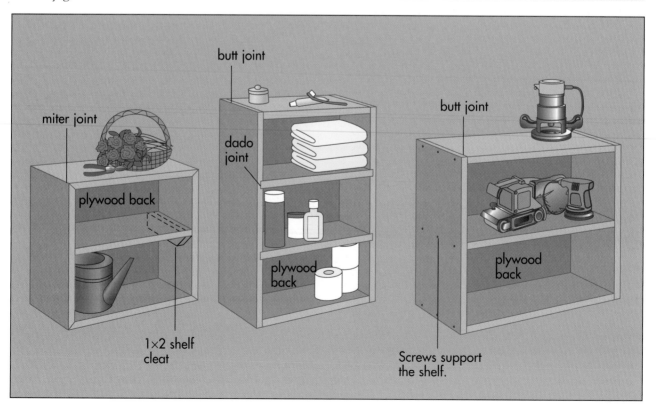

miter joint

butt joint

dado joint

butt joint

plywood back

plywood back

plywood back

1×2 shelf cleat

Screws support the shelf.

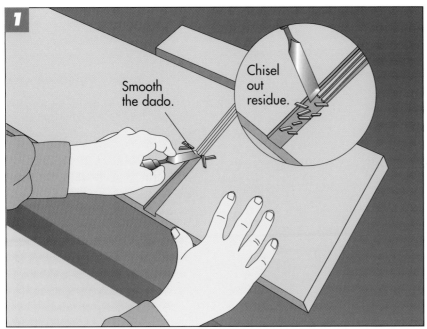

Smooth the dado.

Chisel out residue.

1. Cut outside pieces.

For precise miter cuts, rough cut the outside pieces slightly longer than needed, then cut the miters. Place the two verticals side by side, and clamp them firmly. Draw dado layout lines for each shelf, and use a scrap piece of shelf to make sure you have marked the width correctly. Cut the dadoes $5/16$ inch deep using a circular, radial-arm, or table saw (see pages 38–41). Clean out the dadoes by chiseling out the waste (see inset). Then use the chisel to smooth the bottom of the groove.

Measure dado to dado for shelf length.

Check corners with a framing square.

2. Assemble and measure.

Join the pieces to form a rectangle by drilling pilot holes and driving $2\frac{1}{4}$-inch finish screws. Check for square continually as you fasten. Measure from dado to dado for the lengths of the shelves before cutting the shelves to ensure the best fit.

wood scrap

3. Tap shelves into place.

Carefully slip a shelf into both dadoes. Tap it down using a scrap of wood to keep from marring the shelf edge. Avoid tapping one end down farther than the other; alternate between ends every inch or so or gently tap the middle of the shelf to work it into place. When the shelf edges are flush with the edges of the outside pieces, drill pilot holes and drive screws to reinforce and tighten the joints.

$\frac{1}{4}$" plywood

4d box nails

$\frac{1}{8}$" reveal

4. Add the back.

Cut a piece of $\frac{1}{4}$-inch plywood $\frac{1}{4}$ inch smaller than the shelf unit in both directions. Center it on the back so there is a $\frac{1}{8}$-inch reveal all around. Drive 4d box nails every 6 inches or so.

INSTALLING ADJUSTABLE SHELVES

Inside a frame, support adjustable shelves near each corner and in the middle of the span if needed. The most common method is to use metal support strips with clips, sometimes called pilasters. Attach them to the inside faces of the side pieces, or cut grooves and set them in (see page 57). You can also opt for one of the pin methods shown on page 63.

The important thing is to get all four supports level with each other. Work systematically and double-check often—it's easy to misalign the supports.

The total system.
Space clips as you would other supports (see the chart on page 57). If the span between vertical outside pieces is too great, install a center stile with a support strip attached. The shelf must be wide enough to fit snugly between the stile and the rear support strip.

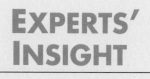

EXPERTS' INSIGHT

TALL UNITS NEED A FIXED SHELF

■ Place support strips on side pieces that are stable and strong; if they warp, the clips may no longer support the shelf. Support strips will add some rigidity, but not much.

■ If the vertical pieces are made of 1-by lumber and are longer than 4 feet, install one fixed shelf about halfway up to ensure that the sides do not bow outward. Attach the shelf with a butt joint or a dado joint (see page 61). Then install support strips or pins above and below the fixed shelf.

YOU'LL NEED

TIME: An hour for support strips; several hours for other methods.
SKILLS: Measuring, drilling, attaching with screws.
TOOLS: Drill, hacksaw, tape measure, square, pegboard.

1. Mark for cutting strips.
Cut one piece to the desired height. It doesn't need to extend to the top of the unit, just a notch or two beyond the top shelf. Use the first piece to measure for the others. Line up the slots. To help position the clips later, line up the numbers as well.

about 1" out

2. Mark and cut dadoes.
Position each strip an inch or so from the edge of the unit, and trace lines. See pages 38–41 for instructions on cutting dadoes. (If you want to set the support strips into dadoes, remember to cut the dadoes before beginning to assemble the shelf unit.)

awl

3. Attach with screws.
Position the support strip and use an awl or sharp pencil to mark for the screws. Drill pilot holes with a drill bit and a depth guide so you won't drill through. A piece of tape wrapped around the drill bit will serve this purpose. Drive screws to attach it.

MEASUREMENTS

TIPS FOR DRILLING A GRID OF PIN HOLES

■ If the shelf unit has one or more vertical dividers in the middle of the unit, avoid placing holes directly opposite each other on the divider, or else the holes will meet and poke all the way through. To prevent this, offset the vertical lines by ½ inch or so.

■ Save yourself time by drilling only as many holes as you really need. The grid need not extend the length of the vertical board. Start at the lowest possible position for the bottom shelf, and end at the highest possible position for the top shelf.

hardwood dowel

bracket pin

flat pin

Pin options.
For an inconspicuous support system, drill holes at regular intervals and insert pins. Metal (or plastic) pins come in two types, a flat pin and a bracket pin. Or cut lengths of hardwood dowel to fit into the holes. When using pins, the shelves must fit tightly; if there is more than a ⅛-inch gap between a shelf and the vertical board, the pin could work itself loose and cause the shelf to fall.

Mark the top.

perforated hardboard

framing square

To space holes, use pegboard...
Cut a piece of perforated hardboard (pegboard) to fit into the space, and use it as a guide. Note which end goes up, so you always align it the same way.

... or use a square.
Draw vertical lines about an inch in from the front and rear edges of the unit. Measure with a framing square or tape measure, and mark evenly spaced horizontal lines at

one of the vertical lines. Then use a square to copy the horizontal measurements onto the other vertical line. Use a drill bit depth guide so you don't drill through the standard.

OTHER SHELF MOUNTING OPTIONS

Anything that supports a board and keeps it level and perpendicular to a wall is a shelf support. When using flexible materials like cable or rope as shelf supports, the challenge is to get the spacing between shelves even. (It's very difficult to get knots in a rope evenly spaced.) Chain links are easier to work with. You can finely tune cable brackets by loosening a setscrew.

When hanging a suspended shelf unit, be sure the hook or bracket is strong enough. And always attach it to a framing member (for example, a stud), not just to the wall material.

Sometimes a specialty shelf can be used for other purposes. In the kitchen department of a home center you can find a number of small shelves designed for the back of cabinet doors; these may be suitable for a workshop or in a child's room.

Chains and bolts.
Buy chain with at least 1-inch-long links, and bolts that fit snugly into the links. Drill holes 2 inches in from each shelf edge. Fasten the threaded hooks into studs so each hook is 2 inches from the wall. Insert bolts into links to support the shelves.

Coated cable and glass.
Sleek plastic covered cables make a modern-style support for a glass shelf. Cable crimps form the loops that attach to a threaded hook. Adhesive clips on the cable hold the shelf horizontal. Glass can be cut to size and edges smoothed at a glass shop.

Sawtooth standards.
This traditional support system will take time and much cutting. Make standards by cutting thirty 60-degree triangles in 1×2s as shown. A professional-quality saber saw will help. Make four standards, and attach two to each side piece. Cut two movable cleats for each shelf. Notch the corners of each shelf so it fits between the standards. Install a plywood back for the unit, and attach a fixed shelf near the middle for rigidity.

MAKING SHELVES FOR CHILDREN

*F*lexibility and durability are the key for children's shelving and storage structures.

Kids grow fast; a shelving system that can adjust in height and function gives the longest service. When possible, make units that can be easily changed, such as the shelf boxes at *right*. This way, children can make it their own by rearranging it to suit their needs.

Pine 1-by is ideal for these shelves. Give it a very durable coat of paint, or stain and finish it so that the inevitable scratches will not be glaring.

YOU'LL NEED

TIME: Several hours for a few boxes; a day for the sports unit.
SKILLS: Measuring and cutting, making dado joints.
TOOLS: Drill, power saw, hammer, tape measure, square.

Modular shelving.
Make a variety of sizes—not only different widths and heights, but different depths as well. The spaces between boxes also can be used for storage, so it is not necessary to plan a system precisely. Construct a box with simple butt joints, then reinforce the corners with 3-inch angle brackets. Cut a piece of ¼-inch plywood for the back, and use it to help square up the box.

Sports organizer.
This keeps sports equipment from cluttering a room. The pegs are handy for hanging gloves, hats, and baseball bats. Large balls go in the lower bin.

Cut and assemble.
Cut side pieces as shown, and cut ⁵⁄₁₆-inch-deep dadoes (see pages 38–41) for the shelves. Cut the shelves and fasten them in the dadoes with 1⅝-inch trimhead screws. Attach the plywood back with 4d box nails. Use a guide to drill ¾-inch holes, 3 inches deep, into the 2×8; insert the dowels. Attach the 2×8 so it overhangs evenly on both sides.

BUILDING A CLASSIC SHELF UNIT

*T*his handsome unit looks elaborate, yet it does not call for extraordinary skills or tools. The shelves are designed for strength: Reinforced with 1×2s on edge, the shelves can span 4 feet even when loaded with a full set of encyclopedias. Use birch plywood to make the sides and the shelves, and pine moldings if you want to paint the unit. If you choose instead to stain, use hardwood 1×10 for the shelves. Select decorative trim along the top and bottom to suit your decor.

YOU'LL NEED

TIME: 1½ days.
SKILLS: Cutting moldings, drilling a grid of holes, attaching with nails and screws.
TOOLS: Drill, square, miter box, tape measure, hammer.

1. Prepare for construction.

The laminated standards are very rigid, so they won't bow out under the pressure of long shelves full of books. To make them, rip-cut pieces of plywood to 11⅛ inches, or use 1×12s. Cut them to the total height of the unit, or cut them a little short and install moldings that increase the height an inch or so.

If the unit will run all the way to the ceiling, attach 1×2 nailers on the ceiling; you'll attach the standards to these. You can then install crown molding or cove molding at the joint between the shelf and the ceiling.

If the unit will not reach to the ceiling, consider installing a piece of plywood or 1-by lumber fitted into the space between the standards, the top face piece, and the wall.

Attach a piece of ½-inch plywood to the back of the unit, or attach the standards directly to the wall.

1×4 — 1×2 — 1×4 — 1×2

1×2

1×12

1×2

1×2

¾" plywood, 11⅛" wide

1×10

2. Make standards.

Lay the outside piece of each standard on a flat surface, then the 1×2s, then the inside piece. Drill pilot holes, using a depth guide so you don't drill through, and drive 2-inch trim head screws spaced about 4 inches apart. Use perforated hardboard as a template to drill holes for bracket pins (see page 63).

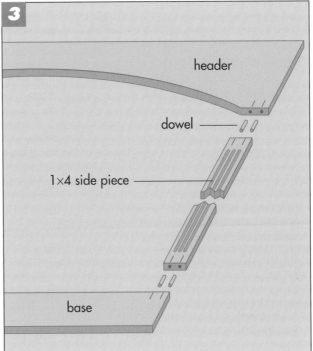

3. Build the face.

Cut the top, bottom, and two side pieces. Draw a long curve along the bottom edge of the top piece, beginning and ending 3½ inches from each end. Cut with a saber saw (see page 27). Working on a large, flat surface, join the side pieces to the top and bottom with blind dowels (see page 37).

4. Install standards, face, and trim.

Have a helper hold the standards upright while you attach the face. The outside edges of the face should be flush with the outside faces of the standards. Drill pilot holes and drive 1⅝-inch trim head screws every 6 inches. Attach a back piece and anchor the back to the wall, or anchor the standards to the wall with angle brackets. Install trim above and below.

5. Make shelves.

Measure the distance between the standards, and cut 9½-inch-wide pieces of plywood or 1×10s for shelves. For each shelf, cut two 1×2 edging pieces as long as the shelf. Attach them to the front and back edges of the shelf with white glue and 6d finish nails. Insert shelving pins into the holes in the standard, and place the shelves in position.

BUILDING A PLATE SHELF

This wall-hung plate shelf is an attractive display piece for a kitchen or eating area. A front lip on the shelves safely holds the plates; 1×1-inch rails in back add a decorative touch and keep the plates from rubbing against the wall. Pegs along the bottom display a collection of mugs.

Pine is a pleasing choice for this informal piece. Stain or a clear finish suits an informal decor; use gloss enamel for easy cleaning if you choose to paint it.

YOU'LL NEED

TIME: Most of a day.
SKILLS: Measuring and cutting, making dado joints, miter-cutting molding.
TOOLS: Circular or table saw, drill, square, tape measure.

Cut pieces and assemble.

Cut the two side pieces to length. Make a template for the bottom curved cut similar to the one shown on page 56, and cut it with a saber saw. Cut $^{5}/_{16}$-inch-deep rabbets at the top, and dadoes for the shelves (see pages 38–41). Cut $^{3}/_{4}$-inch square notches in the back of each side piece for the two rails.

Cut and join the shelves by gluing, drilling pilot holes, and driving 6d nails. Cut the rails to length and attach with glue and nails. (If 1×1 is not available, rip-cut a piece of 1-by lumber to $^{3}/_{4}$ inch.) Cut the 1×3 cup rack to fit between the side pieces. Use a drill with a guide to bore regularly spaced $^{3}/_{4}$-inch holes that angle slightly upward. Buy Shaker pegs or cut pieces of $^{3}/_{4}$-inch dowel to 3 inches and sand the edges smooth. Squeeze some white glue into each hole and tap in the pegs. Attach the cup rack with 6d finish nails driven from the sides. Miter and install the trim.

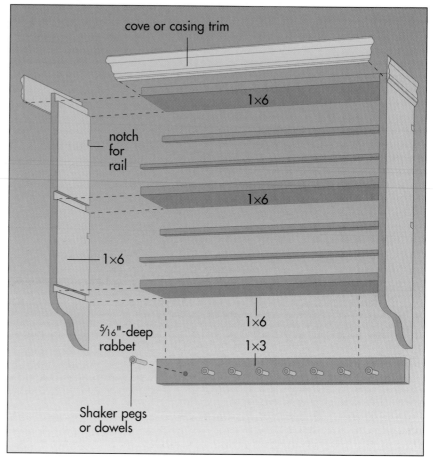

cove or casing trim

notch for rail

1×6

1×6

1×6

$^{5}/_{16}$"-deep rabbet

1×6

1×3

Shaker pegs or dowels

INSTALLING AN ARCHED NICHE

This makes a whimsical alcove for a flower vase or piece of sculpture. It is not so much building a shelf as a reshaping of the wall.

Most wall studs are spaced 16 inches on center, so there is 14½ inches between them, just enough room for the niche. If studs are more closely spaced (as they sometimes are near the end of a wall), or if electrical or plumbing lines run through the space, you will have to find another place for this project.

YOU'LL NEED
TIME: 1 day, plus time for three coats of joint compound to dry.
SKILLS: Cutting, gluing and clamping, patching a wall.
TOOLS: Hammer, crosscut saw, keyhole saw, clamps, wallboard taping knives.

1. Cut the hole.
Locate the wall studs. Drill a small hole and insert an unbent coat hanger to test whether there is enough space or if there is wiring or plumbing behind the space. If there isn't, use a keyhole saw to cut out a rectangle from stud to stud. Install a level 2×4 at the bottom of the hole, toenailing it to the studs.

2. Make the arch.
Nail two 2×4s to a piece of plywood, spaced as far apart as the opening. Cut six long strips of matte board the depth of the wall. Laminate them with carpenter's glue and shape them into an arch. Clamp the sides to the 2×4s and allow the arch to dry. Cut the matte-board arch to proper height.

3. Finish the edge.
Use the arch as a template to mark the wall and cut it out. Insert the arch, then glue it to the studs with construction adhesive. Attach flexible corner bead to the outside edge and drywall tape to the inside edges. Apply several coats of joint compound, sand smooth, and paint to match the wall.

INSTALLING RECESSED SHELVING

Recessed shelves are real space savers, ideal for collectibles and knickknacks. Setting shelves inside a wall looks more difficult than it actually is; checking that the wall cavity is free of electrical and plumbing lines and cutting a clean opening are the most difficult steps. Otherwise you simply build a box shelf (see pages 60–61) and insert it in the wall. The unit shown here spans across two studs. If a unit 14½ inches wide will suit your needs, you can build it without cutting a stud.

YOU'LL NEED
TIME: A full day.
SKILLS: Cutting walls, basic cabinetmaking.
TOOLS: Saber saw, reciprocating saw or keyhole saw, drill, hammer, tape measure, level.

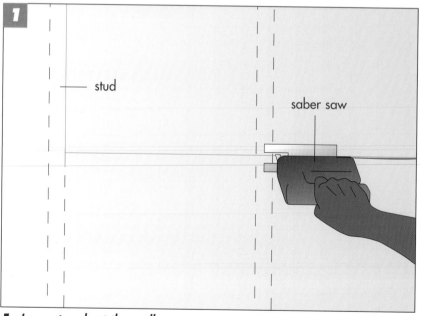

stud

saber saw

1. Lay out and cut the wall.
Locate studs by rapping on the wall, drilling test holes, or using a stud sensor. Drill holes and insert an unbent coat hanger to explore behind the opening. Do not cut the wall if electrical or plumbing lines are between the studs.

Cut the drywall with a saber saw or keyhole saw. (If the wall is plaster, cutting will be difficult: Score lines deeply with a knife first to prevent cracking the surrounding area.) Cut alongside the studs for vertical lines; mark horizontal cut lines with a level.

CAUTION!
IS IT A LOAD-BEARING WALL?
Some interior walls are simply partitions between rooms. Others are "load-bearing," meaning that they support the roof or a wall on the floor above. Walls that run parallel to joists above are not usually load-bearing. Outside walls are load-bearing, and walls that run perpendicular to overhead joists may be load-bearing as well. Check by taking measurements to see whether a wall above is directly on top of the wall you want to cut into. Do not cut a stud of a load-bearing wall. Consult with a carpenter if you are not sure.

Wedge a 2×4 into place.

2. Cut the stud and install the sill.

Use a reciprocating saw to cut the center stud at the bottom and the top. Or cut as deeply as you can with a circular saw, then finish the cut with a handsaw. Be careful not to cut through the wall surface on the other side. Cut a 2×4 sill to the width of the opening, and attach it with screws. Make sure it is level.

bar clamp

holes for bracket pins

3. Build the recessed unit.

Build a shelf unit like this butt-jointed frame with adjustable shelves resting on support pins (see pages 32 and 63). Rip-cut the boards to the depth of the opening, less ¼ inch for the back piece. Make the unit ½ inch smaller than the opening on all sides. Before assembling, drill holes for bracket pins.

shim

4. Install shelf unit in the opening.

Set the unit in place. Check for level and plumb, and make sure the front edge is flush with the wall surface. Use shims if necessary. Drill pilot holes and drive 6d finish nails through the sides and bottom; drive one nail through the top into the cut stud.

4d finishing nail

6d finishing nail

5. Trim it out.

Install molding around the perimeter. Butt-jointed casing is the simplest, although you may prefer to miter the corners. Drill pilot holes to avoid cracking the wood, and drive 6d nails into studs and 4d nails into the shelf unit.

ADDING UNDER-STAIR SHELVES

The area under a basement stairway often goes to waste; stacking boxes there is awkward because the space is triangular. A shelf system provides a convenient place to store canned goods, bulk purchases, and sports equipment.

Because basement floors may become damp, the bottom shelf should be raised a bit by resting it on pressure-treated 2×4 sleepers, which will not rot even if they get soaked occasionally.

Rather than measuring each upright individually—a complicated process—the technique shown here allows you to quickly cut the outline of the triangle, then make shelves to fit.

YOU'LL NEED

TIME: Most of a day.
SKILLS: Careful measuring, making bevel cuts, fastening with screws.
TOOLS: Power saw, drill, level, framing square, chalk line.

Under-stair shelves.
Basic shelves like these can be quickly assembled with screws. Offset the shelves so they do not line up horizontally; that way, you will be able to drive screws straight through the uprights and into the shelves. For a more finished look and for greater strength, you can set the shelves in dadoes (see pages 38–41), cut into the uprights.

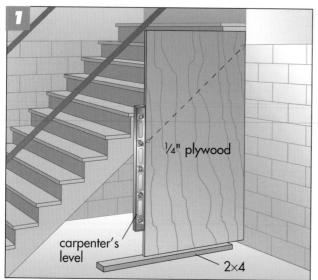

1. Mark and cut backing plywood.
Place a piece of ¼-inch plywood against the stairway, resting it on top of a piece of 2×4, positioned along the stairway where it will be at the back of the shelves. Be sure to check for plumb before measuring and marking. Mark each side, snap a chalk line, and cut. Do the same for the other backing pieces.

2. Lay out on the backing pieces.
Test to see that the backing pieces fit. Then lay them down and draw layout lines indicating shelves and uprights. Step up each shelf ¾ inch so you can fasten each from the side. Avoid making unusably small triangular shelves. The shelves will be wide; use ¾-inch plywood so they won't sag.

3. Bevel-cut the pieces.

The uprights should be bevel-cut at an angle, where they meet the stringer, and the shelves at another angle. Hold a T-bevel against the plywood backing pieces to find the correct angle, and transfer that angle to a circular saw, table saw, or radial arm saw. Cut the pieces to width. Measure the layout lines, and cut all shelves and uprights to length. Then cut the bevels.

4. Attach sleepers to the floor.

Cut two pieces of pressure-treated 2×4 to fit along the bottom of the shelf system. Attach them to a concrete floor with 2-inch masonry nails every foot or so.

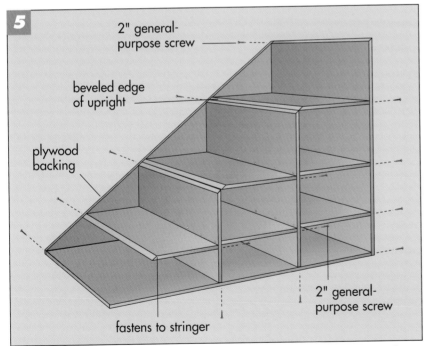

5. Assemble the shelf unit.

Place the shelves and uprights on the backing pieces to make sure they are correctly cut. Use a framing square to line up the shelves. Attach the components by driving 2-inch general-purpose screws every few inches at each joint. Check for square continually, and make sure none of the pieces extends beyond the plywood backing. Slide the assembled unit into place, and fasten the beveled shelf edges to the stringer.

EXPERTS' INSIGHT

BUILDING WIDE PLYWOOD SHELVES

■ Plywood can soak up a lot of paint, making for a costly and time-consuming job. Consider covering the shelf tops with shelf paper, and giving the other surfaces a quick coat of polyurethane. If you choose to paint, birch-veneer plywood soaks up less paint than pine.

■ Whenever cutting across the surface grain of plywood, first score the cut line with a utility knife to prevent splintering. You do not need to do this when cutting with the grain.

■ Give exposed plywood edges a quick sanding with a hand sander to remove burrs and to prevent splinters from developing.

BUILDING UTILITY SHELVES AND RACKS

Utilitarian shelves and racks for a workshop or garage can be made of unfinished plywood and 2-bys. Locate them so lumber and sheet goods can be easily stacked and removed. Make some shelves deep enough for your largest items, and others shallower so cans of paint don't get lost in the back. Before you buy lumber to build your own unit, check the storage options at a home center. Ladder brackets (*right*) and metal shelf units are often more cost-effective than shelves built from scratch.

YOU'LL NEED

TIME: Half a day or less for any of these projects
SKILLS: Basic measuring, cutting, and fastening skills.
TOOLS: Power saw, drill, square, level, chalk line.

Store-bought ladder brackets.
Ready-made ladder brackets are available at most home centers and will probably cost little more than homemade. Have helpers hold the ladder brackets plumb while you attach ¾-inch plywood shelving with screws. Anchor the unit to the wall with angle brackets and screws driven into studs.

1. Assemble the lumber racks.
Cut 3-inch-wide strips of plywood and assemble them into a U shape, using mending plates and ¾-inch screws to join them.

2. Hang the racks.
Chalk a line on the underside of the joists so that the racks will be in line with each other. Attach the the tops of the racks to joists by driving four 2-inch screws through each of the plywood supports and into the joists. Stack the lumber neatly, putting the widest pieces on the bottom to support the other boards and to keep them from warping.

Shelves and plywood storage.

This arrangement will keep sheet goods easily accessible and prevent them from warping. Build standard shelves with 2×2 uprights and 1×2 horizontal supports. Make the bottom plywood channel out of two 1×4s and one 1×2; drill pilot holes and drive screws to fasten them into a U-shape. Drill a hole in the middle of the 1×2 and tie a rope to it. Use the rope to hold sheets of plywood securely in place.

Hanging jars.

Your grandfather may have used this system to organize screws and small items, and it still works. Drive screws to fasten jar lids to the underside of a shelf, and screw the jar onto the lid.

Between-joist rack.

Use the space between open joists in a garage or basement to store lumber, pipes, or other long objects. Attach 1×2s to the underside of the joists for an instant rack. If the stored objects will be heavy, attach 2×4s instead of 1×2s.

Over-joist storage platform.

If your garage or attic has space above the joists, slide pieces of ½-inch plywood up there, and attach them to the joists with 1¼-inch screws. Make the platform roomy, and leave enough empty space on the sides so you can easily get to all the stored objects.

LAYING OUT KITCHEN CABINETS

Use your present cabinets as a starting place for planning the storage you need. Are your pans crammed into one cabinet? Plan to move them near the cooktop and store them in built-in pullout shelves. Can you store all your dishware near the dishwasher? Plan so items can be stored close to where they're used.

Kitchen designers talk about the "work triangle"—the path between the cooktop, the refrigerator, and the sink and dishwasher. Preferably, this triangle should be away from kitchen traffic patterns. The total distance should be between 12 and 27 feet; each leg of the work triangle should be from 4 to 9 feet.

Standard kitchen base cabinets are 34½ inches tall and 22 inches deep so the countertop will be 36 inches high and 24 inches deep. Wall cabinets are usually 12 inches deep and may be 30, 36, or 42 inches tall. The bottom of a wall cabinet is usually 18 inches above the countertop—54 inches above the floor.

An island can be made from a standard base cabinet: Cover the unfinished sides with plywood that matches the rest of the cabinets.

Refrigerator dimensions affect layout: Side-by-side models can be up to 35 inches wide and 69 inches tall; single-door models are 30 to 32 inches wide and up to 67 inches tall. Both leave room for a short wall cabinet above. Or, you can install cabinet-like 27-inch-wide modular refrigerators.

EXPERTS' INSIGHT

WORK ORDER

Every cabinet installation is unique, but the major stages should proceed in this order:
- Demolition and removal of existing cabinets; rough wiring, plumbing, and ductwork.
- Patching and priming walls; installing flooring.
- Installing cabinets; finish painting; countertops.
- Finish plumbing and electrical—sink, dishwasher, cooktop, oven, range hood.

length | hood

W2836 | W2436 | W3015 | W2436 | W2036 | CB36

B28 | DB24 | DB24 | B15

30" refrigerator | 30" range

B18 | W2436

door | SB36 | width | window

30" dishwasher | B18 | W2436

B28 | B15 | W2036 | CB36

sliding doors | window

Draw up a plan.

Begin by making your own plan with graph paper, tracing paper, pencil, and a straightedge. Make the drawing to scale—for instance, have each graph paper square equal 4 inches. Measure your kitchen carefully. Check to see that walls are plumb and square; if not, you may have an inch less space than you think. Draw the basic floor plan on graph paper, then overlay tracing paper to try out different cabinet layouts.

Some cabinet retailers have computer programs to help design your project. The programs even show you what the cabinets will look like from various angles—and what the cabinets will cost. If you have access to a design computer, your plan will provide essential dimensions and give you a head start on the design.

Use these standard cabinet designations: B (base cabinet), W (wall cabinet), DB (drawer base), WC (corner wall cabinet), CB (corner base cabinet), SB (sink base). Dimensions (in inches) come after these designations. The first number refers to width, and the second refers to height. Base cabinets are always $34\frac{1}{2}$ inches tall, so they have only one number: the width. For example, "DB18" means a drawer base 18 inches wide; "W3036" is a wall cabinet 30 inches wide and 36 inches tall.

If you build your own cabinets, you can make them any size you want. Manufactured cabinets come in a limited number of standard sizes, so you will have to choose an ensemble of different sizes that fit the space.

Place cabinets where they are most convenient. For instance, position a drawer base for silverware near the dishwasher, and put a large base cabinet for pots and pans near the range. Do not plan for cabinets to fit tightly, or you may not be able to squeeze them all in. Allow room for a 1- to 3-inch spacer at the end of every run. Leave plenty of room for your range and refrigerator; they should not fit too snugly. Check manufacturers' recommendations for openings.

Plan for furniture as well as cabinets. In the example *above*, there is just enough room for a table with chairs.

CHOOSING CABINETS

While the decorating style of cabinets can vary widely, there are just a few essential configurations. Storage accessories (see pages 90–91) can be added to suit your storage requirements.

When considering these configurations, remember that the doors should swing open in directions that allow for easy access.

Base cabinets have toe spaces 3½ to 4 inches high and 3 inches deep so you can stand next to the countertop comfortably. The most common base cabinet has a single drawer on top and two shelves below. If the cabinet is wider than 24 inches, it will have two drawers and two doors. You may be able to save money by buying a few larger cabinets instead of several smaller cabinets. Most kitchens need at least one drawer base. Make sure that the sink base has enough room for the sink and its plumbing.

Sometimes the layout will call for a shallow base cabinet, to allow for the swing of a back door, for example. Use a 30-inch-tall wall cabinet (which is 12 inches deep). Set it on 1×4s (¾×3½ inches in actual dimension) to mimic the toe space of standard base cabinets, and add a 1-inch spacer on top.

Tall wall cabinets provide more storage space for not much more money; but if you can't reach the top shelf, it may not be of much use. Most people prefer 30- or 36-inch-tall wall cabinets, although 40-inch-tall cabinets are available.

Corner cabinets have hard-to-reach spaces; a lazy Susan in either a wall or a base corner cabinet may be the solution.

For maximum storage where you do not need a countertop, install a pantry cabinet.

A spacer for a wall cabinet is just a piece of 1-by lumber stained to match the cabinet. A spacer for a base cabinet includes a toe kick.

Framed and frameless cabinets. Framed cabinets usually have 1×2 frame pieces to provide rigidity. Frameless cabinets rely on the cabinet walls for strength. Framed cabinets allow for a variety of hinge types; frameless cabinets have Euro-style hinges (see page 44).

Frameless cabinets offer a cleaner look and use space more efficiently. However, you must use spacers in corners so that the doors can open completely.

Framed cabinets offer a more traditional appearance, are stronger overall, and are easier to install. However, both the door and drawer openings are smaller than those in frameless cabinets.

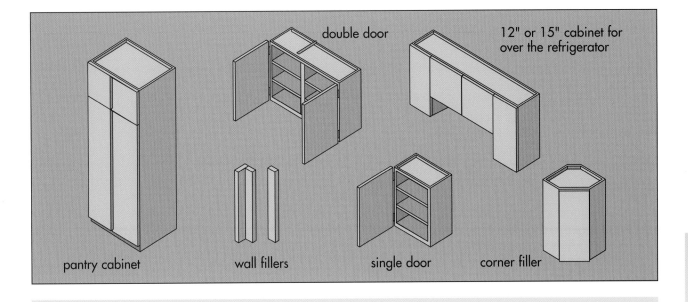

double door

12" or 15" cabinet for over the refrigerator

pantry cabinet

wall fillers

single door

corner filler

PURCHASING OPTIONS FOR KITCHEN CABINETS

If you want to buy kitchen cabinets, choose from the following purchasing strategies.

■ Ready-to-assemble (RTA) and unfinished cabinets are usually the least-expensive option. You can find these stacked on large shelves in home centers. They take some time to assemble and/or finish, but they may be worth the trouble. Be sure you can purchase fillers, wire racks, and other amenities that will fit the brand you choose. Unfinished cabinets offer savings, but be realistic about your ability to achieve a consistent finish.

■ Stock preassembled cabinets range from 9 to 48 inches in width, in 3-inch increments. Most large manufacturers have a catalog that lists cabinet types and amenities. You will have a limited number of finishes and colors to choose from. Watch prices carefully—often the basic cabinets are reasonable, but prices climb on special cabinet inserts and amenities. Some makers can deliver cabinets within a week.

■ Semi-custom cabinets are built to your exact specifications by the manufacturer. This lets you get cabinets that fit your space

exactly, and you can choose your finish. However, style choices may be limited. Also, you'll have to allow weeks or months for delivery. Even less convenient, you'll face a long wait for a replacement if a cabinet is damaged in transit.

■ Custom cabinets are the most expensive. They are measured on site by the fabricator and made locally, which might mean less wait than with semi-custom cabinets. Also, in most cases, custom cabinets offer the largest selection of finishes and styles to choose from.

CABINET MATERIALS

Take a close look at the cabinets you are considering. Solid wood is usually used for cabinet frames, and sometimes for doors, but rarely for the main body of cabinets. Often cabinets are made of a combination of materials.

■ A word of caution about particleboard: This "engineered" wood is made by bonding wood fiber with resin. If the material is not well reinforced with solid materials, it

will lack strength. Overlong particleboard shelves will sag over time. High-quality particleboard, rated as 45-pound commercial grade, is better than standard; but no particleboard holds fasteners well.

■ Medium-density fiberboard (MDF) has a harder surface than particleboard and will take paint more readily. But it is no stronger than particleboard; hinges should be attached to solid wood frames.

■ Laminates vary in quality. Standard plastic laminates, such as those used on countertops, are strong. Other products, such as melamine, are easily chipped. All laminates are difficult to repair.

■ Plywood, made by laminating thin layers (plies) of wood together, is the best material for structural support. It is very strong, is almost impossible to crack, and takes finishes well.

BUILDING A BASE CABINET

Professional cabinetmakers make detailed drawings and figure the dimensions for all of the cabinet components before making the first cut. Follow their example: It's the only way to ensure against costly cutting mistakes, and it will save you time in the long run.

Planning cabinet construction requires three steps. First, make *scaled drawings* of the project on graph paper. Then make a *cut list* spelling out the exact dimensions of all the parts. Finally, draw a *cutting diagram* that shows how you will cut out all the pieces.

YOU'LL NEED

TIME: Most cabinets can be built in a day.
SKILLS: Accurate measuring and cutting; squaring, fastening.
TOOLS: Power saw, drill, square, hammer, and nail set.

Scaled drawings, cutting diagram. The scaled drawings (*above*) and the cutting diagram (*below*) are for a base cabinet 33 inches wide, 24 inches deep, and 34½ inches high. Be sure the plywood grain runs up and down for the side pieces. You may have to redraw and refigure several times before all of the dimensions come out right.

1. Build the base.

Cut the base pieces to the specified sizes. Working on a flat surface, attach the pieces together by drilling pilot holes, applying wood glue, and driving three 8d finish nails at each joint. Periodically check the frame for square as you work. Align the sides with the notched kick plate as shown on the drawing.

2. Cut and attach the sides.

Cut the cabinet sides, then notch the front edge of each to fit over the notch in the kick plate. Rabbet the back edge of each side piece to accommodate the 1/4-inch plywood back (see pages 38–39). Drill pilot holes, glue, and drive 8d finish nails to attach the sides to the base.

3. Install the bottom shelf.

Cut the bottom shelf to size, and test to see that it fits between the sides. Apply glue to the top edge of the base pieces, and set the shelf in place. Be sure its front edge is flush with the fronts of the sides. Drill pilot holes and drive 6d finish nails through the shelf and into the base.

4. Cut and install the ledger.

Double-check the length of the ledger by measuring the distance between the inside edges of the cabinet sides at the bottom of the cabinet. Cutting to this length will ensure that the cabinet is square. Attach the ledger with 8d finish nails; position it so the back piece can slip into the rabbet.

5. Install the plywood back.

Cut a piece of ¼-inch plywood to fit between the rabbets. Take care to cut it perfectly square. It does not need to extend down to the floor, but it must cover the entire back opening. Test fit it, and check that the cabinet is square. Drive several 4d finish nails partway through it near the edges. Lay a bead of wood glue in the rabbet on both sides, and fasten with nails driven every few inches.

6. Fit in the center divider.

Cabinets wider than 24 inches need two doors and two drawers, so there must be a center divider. Cut a piece of ¾-inch plywood so its front aligns with the front edge of the bottom and its top edge aligns with the top. Make a notch to accommodate the ledger. Position the divider in the center of the cabinet, and attach with 8d finish nails and wood glue.

7. Add the shelves.

A base cabinet shelf is usually 6 inches or so shallower than the bottom so that you can reach the pots and pans in the bottom compartment. Cut shelves to fit. Use a framing square to mark the location of the shelves, and attach them with wood glue and 8d finish nails.

8. Add the face frame and front cross pieces.

Cut four plywood front crosspieces, and attach them with glue and 8d finish nails. Cut the vertical stiles, and install them with nails and glue, positioning the outer ones so they extend ⅛ inch past each side of the cabinet. Cut the horizontal rails to fit between the stiles, and fasten them as well. Now you are ready for drawers and doors (see pages 42–49).

BUILDING A WALL CABINET

Because it has no kick plate or drawers, a wall cabinet is easier to build than a base cabinet. It is essentially a rectangular box with shelves and a face frame. Build a standard wall cabinet 12 inches deep, including the stiles and rails but not including the doors.

Base cabinets usually have one fixed shelf, but wall cabinets work well with two or three adjustable shelves. Make scaled drawings, a cut list, and a cutting diagram (see page 80).

YOU'LL NEED

TIME: Several hours per cabinet.
SKILLS: Accurate planning, measuring, cutting, fastening.
TOOLS: Power saw, drill, framing square, hammer.

Making the cabinet.

Cut the sides to the total height of the cabinet. Install adjustable standards, or drill a grid of holes for shelf pins (see pages 62–63). For each side piece, cut a ³/₄ × ³/₈-inch rabbet at the top, a ³/₄ × ³/₈-inch dado for the bottom shelf, and a ³/₈ × ³/₈-inch rabbet for the back panel (see pages 38–41).

Cut the bottom shelf and the top 1 inch shorter than the width of the cabinet, and cut a ³/₈ × ³/₈-inch rabbet in the rear of the top piece. Fasten together the sides, the top piece, and the bottom shelf using wood glue and 8d finish nails. Check for square as you work.

Cut the back from ¹/₄-inch plywood, ³/₄ inch narrower than the width of the cabinet and ³/₈ inch shorter than the cabinet's height. Cut carefully so that all corners are square. Cut and fasten the top and bottom cleats. Squeeze wood glue onto the back rabbet, and attach the back by driving 3d finish nails every few inches.

³/₈" × ³/₈" rabbet · top · cleat · ³/₈" × ³/₄" rabbet · ¹/₄" plywood back · side · screen molding · adjustable standards · cleat · bottom · 1" · stile · rail

Cut the stiles (the vertical pieces of the face frame) to the height of the cabinet and cut the rails (horizontal pieces) to fit between. Hold in place on the cabinet front to check the cuts; the stiles should extend ¹/₈ inch on each side. For the tightest joints, square up and glue the stiles and rails together before fastening them to the cabinet. Attach the completed face frame using wood glue and 8d finish nails.

Cut shelves to fit inside the cabinet. Make them ¹/₈ inch shorter than the opening so you can remove and reposition them easily. Cover the front edges of the shelves with screen molding (see page 50).

To build and hang a cabinet door, see pages 42–47.

BUILDING SPECIAL BASE CABINETS

Base cabinets hold a great deal because they are deep, but cookware and small appliances can get lost in the back corners. Plan for easy access. A narrow base cabinet works well for cookie sheets and baking pans, for instance. Page 89 shows a simpler corner base that uses the kitchen walls for a back. This version includes a finished back to cover imperfections in the wall.

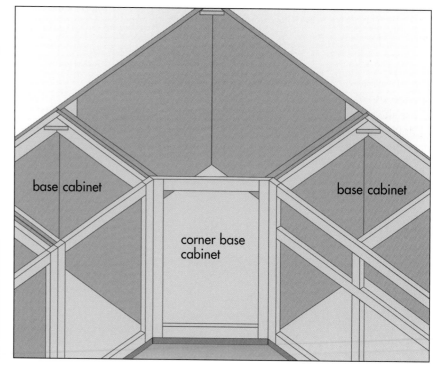

base cabinet

base cabinet

corner base cabinet

YOU'LL NEED

TIME: A few hours
SKILLS: Measuring, marking and cutting; fastening with screws.
TOOLS: Level, power saw, framing square, drill.

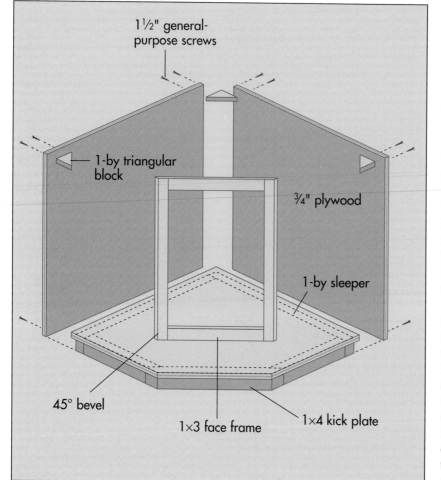

1½" general-purpose screws

1-by triangular block

¾" plywood

1-by sleeper

45° bevel

1×3 face frame

1×4 kick plate

Build a corner base cabinet.

Set base cabinets in place on each side of the corner; level them and make sure they are level with each other, but do not attach them.

Cut ¾-inch plywood for the back, and attach triangular blocks to the outside edge of each, near the top. Attach the back pieces to the wall. Cut a piece of plywood for the bottom. Cut 2-by sleepers to the width needed to raise the bottom of the base to the same height as the adjoining cabinets. Screw the two rear sleepers to the back pieces, and set the other two in place. Fasten the bottom to the sleepers with screws.

Cut a 1×4 to fit between the toe kicks of the adjoining cabinets; make 45-degree bevel cuts at both ends. Attach it with screws. Position the adjoining cabinets against the corner base so the opening between them is square. Construct a face frame of 1×3s to fit tightly in the opening; bevel the outside edges at 45 degrees. Attach the face by drilling pilot holes and driving screws.

Build a drawer base.

A drawer base is similar to a standard base cabinet, but with extra drawers and no doors. Most people prefer to have a larger drawer at the bottom. This version includes a pull-out cutting board. You can build a large cabinet like the one shown on pages 80–82 and make one side a drawer base.

Make drawings and cut lists, and construct the basic frame for the cabinet (see Steps 1–5 on pages 80–82). Install three front crosspieces; the two lower ones should be evenly spaced below the top one, while leaving a larger opening for the bottom drawer. Install nailers and drawer glides for all three drawers.

You don't want the cutting board to slide too smoothly, so provide two cleats on each side for the board to slide between. Make four cleats by rip-cutting pieces of 1-by to ¾ inch, so each is square in profile. Attach the cleats as shown, with a consistent 1-inch space between them.

Make the cutting board out of a hardwood, like maple. It should be ¼ inch narrower than the opening. Join two or three pieces side-by-side with blind dowels or biscuits (see pages 36–37). Then cut a front piece out of 1×2 and join it the same way. Attach a small wooden knob to the front of the cutting board using a double-threaded screw.

Cut stiles, square up, glue and clamp them together, and attach them with 8d finish nails and wood glue. Position the stiles so they overlap the cabinet ⅛ inch on each side. Cut four rails to fit, and install them the same way. To build and install the drawers, see pages 48–49.

BUILDING A PANTRY CABINET

To maximize storage space in an area where you do not need a countertop, build a tall unit that mimics an old-fashioned pantry. This pantry cabinet has a tall space below that you can use as a broom closet; or install adjustable shelves. It is 24 inches deep, but a 12-inch unit will provide plenty of storage where space is at a premium. To store seldom-needed objects, build a pantry cabinet that extends to the ceiling.

YOU'LL NEED

TIME: Most of a day.
SKILLS: Measuring and cutting, cutting dadoes, fastening with screws and nails.
TOOLS: Power saw, drill, framing square, hammer.

If the unit will stand next to standard base and wall cabinets with a countertop, plan so that the top doors match the wall cabinet doors. An 84-inch-tall pantry cabinet will be the same height as 30-inch-tall wall cabinets that are installed 18 inches above the countertop (see page 76).

This unit is made with many of the same techniques shown for a base cabinet (see pages 80–82).

Buy warp-free plywood for the doors and store the pieces flat before cutting. Edge the doors with veneer tape (see page 50) and surface mount trim with glue and brads. Use two catches for the lower doors, one near the bottom and one near the top, to help prevent them from warping over the years.

1×4 cleat

3/8" rabbet

1/4" plywood

kick plate

face frame

surface-applied decorative trim

Building a pantry unit.

Cut the sides, and make 3/4 × 3/8-inch dado cuts for the three fixed shelves (see pages 38-41). Cut a 3/8 × 3/8-inch rabbet at the inside rear edge of each side piece. Install metal standards, or drill a grid of holes for adjustable pins (see pages 62–63).

Cut the three shelves 1 inch shorter than the cabinet width. Working on a flat surface and checking for square, attach the shelves to the side pieces with wood glue and 8d finish nails. Cut a notched kickplate, and attach it with glue and finish nails. Cut 1×4 nailing cleats to fit between the side pieces at the top and bottom, and attach them.

Cut the back panel out of 1/4-inch plywood, making sure each corner is square. Place it inside the rabbets and attach it with wood glue and 3d finish nails every few inches. Attach the stiles with glue and 8d finish nails so that they extend past the side pieces 1/8 inch on each side. Cut and attach rails to fit between them.

MAKING AN ADJUSTABLE SPICE RACK

Adjustable shelves make this more versatile than the usual spice rack. An open rack located near the stove will be convenient while cooking. Many spice containers, bottles of oil, and condiment jars are attractive enough to display.

Choose a hardwood lumber and plywood, and stain it to match your kitchen cabinets; or use softwood, and give it several coats of enamel paint.

YOU'LL NEED

TIME: Half a day.
SKILLS: Measuring and cutting, cutting dadoes, fastening with screws and nails.
TOOLS: Power saw, drill, framing square, hammer.

1. Cut and dado the sides.
Cut two pieces of 1×4 to the height of the unit, minus ¾ inch. Clamp them together, and cut ⅜ × ⅜-inch dadoes, every 2 inches. Leave 2 inches clear at the top and bottom. Cut pieces of 1×4 for the top and bottom, and cut ⅜ × ¾-inch rabbets at both ends of each.

⅜"×⅜" rabbet

¼" plywood back

2. Assemble the parts.
Apply wood glue and clamp the top and bottom pieces to the side pieces, checking for square. When the glue is dry, cut a piece of ¼-inch plywood, ¼ inch shorter and narrower than the unit. Attach it to the back with wood glue and 3d finish nails.

¾" lattice

⅜" plywood

3. Make the shelves.
Cut strips of ⅜-inch plywood, 3½ inches wide, to fit. Measure from dado to dado for the correct length. Glue pieces of ¾-inch lattice molding (which is ¼ inch thick) to the front edge of the shelves, overhanging the shelf edge by about ⅛ inch on each side.

INSTALLING KITCHEN CABINETS

Install cabinets after you complete the rough plumbing and electrical wiring and install the flooring. Patch and prime the walls and give them a first coat of paint before installing cabinets.

If you purchased your cabinets ready-made, inspect them carefully before installing. It is not unusual to find imperfections. Before installing base cabinets, use a level to find the highest point of the floor, and begin the layout from there. When installing wall cabinets, work with a helper and a stable ladder so one person can hold a cabinet in perfect alignment while the other drives screws. Attach cabinets with screws driven at least 2 inches into studs.

YOU'LL NEED

TIME: A full day to install about a dozen cabinets.
SKILLS: Leveling, measuring, attaching with screws.
TOOLS: Level, drill, hammer, clamps, chisel.

1. Lay out for the cabinets.
Installation will go smoothly and you'll have fewer mishaps if you mark the wall to show where each cabinet will go. Also, draw lines to show the stud locations. (Draw lightly wherever your marks will not be covered by a cabinet.) Remove any moldings or other obstructions that would keep cabinets from fitting tightly against the wall.

2. Install wall cabinets.
Begin in a corner. Mark sure that the first wall cabinet is plumb in all directions; use shims if necessary. Drive screws into studs to attach. Secure other cabinets to the wall and to each other (see Step 5).

3. Use a spacer at the end.
At the end of a wall, you may have to rip-cut a spacer at an angle to make it fit snugly. Test-fit the final cabinet and spacer. Clamp the spacer while you drill pilot holes and drive screws.

EXPERTS' INSIGHT

PLUMB AND LEVEL

If the walls or floors are not level or plumb, you may be tempted to "cheat" a little and install cabinets out of level. This is a bad idea: If you start out wrong, the misalignments will be compounded and impossible to correct. If the floor is wavy or out of level, install vinyl cove base to cover up the gap at the bottom of base cabinets. Or you can remove the kick plates and reinstall them tight to the floor after the cabinets are installed.

4. Level and attach base cabinets.

Starting in a corner, set the first base cabinet in place and use shims at the floor or wall (or both) to make it level and plumb in all directions. The cabinet should be resting firmly, with no wobbles, before you attach it. Drive screws through the rear ledger and into studs. Recheck for level and plumb; driving the screws can move the cabinet a bit.

5. Join cabinets together.

Clamp cabinets together so the stiles are flush, and join them by drilling pilot holes and driving screws. Use a chisel to nip off any shims that stick out.

6. Make a simple base cabinet.

If the walls are in good condition, buy a knock-down corner unit like this, or make your own (see page 84 for a unit with backing). Install the base first, aligning the kick plate with those adjoining. Join the face frame to the adjoining cabinets, and install 1×2 cleats on the walls.

7. Install an island.

If a cabinet does not attach to a wall, provide framing on the floor. Measure the inside of the cabinet bottom, and attach 2×4 cleats to the floor so the cabinet can slip over them and fit snugly. Drill pilot holes and drive finish nails, or attach with screws and cover the screw heads with molding.

EXPERTS' INSIGHT

INSTALLATION TIPS

■ If a run of cabinets ends with a dishwasher, purchase or make a plywood end panel (stained to match the cabinets) to go between the dishwasher and the wall. Attach it to the floor, wall, and countertops, using short screws and angle brackets.

■ Durable cabinets that can stand up to decades of normal use can be easily scratched or dinged by carpentry tools. Be careful not to damage cabinets as you work on them. Cover installed cabinets with heavy dropcloths or cardboard from the shipping boxes, and keep sharp tools well away from door and drawer faces.

IMPROVING KITCHEN CABINETS

Raw storage capacity is often undone by awkward access; canned goods get buried, pots and pans get jumbled together. By adding a pull-out drawer, a door-mounted shelf, or small open shelves, you will greatly improve your cabinet's efficiency. Home centers and kitchen supply sources carry many coated-wire racks and shelves, as well as slide-out drawers, that can easily be attached to cabinet doors and floors. Here are three solutions that you can add to new or existing cabinets.

YOU'LL NEED

TIME: About half a day for each project.
SKILLS: Measuring, squaring, cutting dadoes, attaching with screws and nails.
TOOLS: Power saw, drill, hammer, square, chisel.

1. Measure for door-mounted shelves.
To store small items within easy reach, build a shelf system with at least ¾ inch clearance all around the door so the shelves will not bump into the frame.

2. Cut and assemble the pieces.
Cut dadoes in the side pieces, both for the shelves and the stops. Attach the pieces by drilling pilot holes, applying glue, and driving 4d finishing nails. Anchor the unit with screws and angle brackets.

Side-of-cabinet open shelves.
This simple design uses 1×1 cleats against the wall for extra support. Use plywood and cover the edges with molding or veneer tape, or purchase ½-inch-thick lumber for the shelves.

Assemble with dadoes and screws.
Cut ¼ × ½-inch dadoes in the upright support (see pages 38–41). Cut the shelves and attach them in the dadoes with glue and 2½-inch screws driven through the back of the support into the shelves. Drill pilot holes; drive the screws carefully. Cover the shelf edges with ½-inch screen molding, and the support edge with ¾-inch screen molding. Mount the unit by driving screws from inside the cabinet.

1. Roll-out drawers.

Drawers like these greatly increase base cabinet efficiency, allowing you to reach pots and pans, lids, and small appliances without getting down on your knees. Begin by measuring the opening and subtracting the thickness of the glides you'll use.

2. Cut the pieces.

Cut 1×4 sides 22 inches long, and cut $\frac{1}{2} \times \frac{3}{8}$-inch grooves, with the bottom of the grooves $\frac{3}{4}$ inch up from the bottom edge (see pages 38–41). Cut a front and back piece, each to the width of the drawer. Cut grooves in these pieces to match the grooves in the side pieces. Also cut $\frac{3}{8} \times \frac{3}{4}$-inch rabbets on the inside ends of the front and back. Use a saber saw to cut a decorative scallop in the front piece. Cut a piece of $\frac{1}{2}$-inch plywood to fit inside the grooves of the side, back, and front pieces. Install any reinforcement needed for the glide.

3. Assemble and install.

Dry-fit all the pieces to make sure that all the joints will be snug. Apply glue to the rabbets (but not to the grooves), drill pilot holes, and attach all the joints with 4d finish nails. Attach nailers to the insides of the cabinets, and install glides on both the nailers and the drawer (see page 49).

EXPERTS' INSIGHT

GETTING THE RIGHT DRAWER SIZES

Before you start building a slide-out drawer for a base cabinet, make sure that it will slide out without bumping into the doors. Some doors provide an opening just as big as the cabinet frame when they open; others provide less space.

If you need to narrow the drawer so that it can slide past the door, you may need to increase the thickness of the glide reinforcement inside the cabinet. Add a strip of $\frac{1}{2}$-inch plywood behind the nailer.

BUILDING ADJUSTABLE ENTERTAINMENT SHELVES

These shelves have an informal look, but if you finish them with a solid covering of enamel paint, or build with oak plywood and stain, they will be classy enough for most living rooms.

The shelves are made of plywood, cut at a gentle curve and edged with veneer tape. The standards are made of 2-inch galvanized conduit, the kind used for heavy-duty outdoor electrical installations. Conduit couplings support the shelves.

YOU'LL NEED

TIME: Several hours, plus time for painting or finishing.
SKILLS: Measuring and cutting curves, cutting metal conduit.
TOOLS: Sabersaw, drill, hammer, framing square, hacksaw.

1. Cut the shelves.

On a sheet of plywood, draw lines for a 6-foot-long, 14-inch-wide curved shelf. Use a framing square and pencil to divide part of the plywood sheet into a grid of 6-inch squares. Then draw the top curve, using the illustration *above* as a guide. Experiment until it looks smooth and even. Draw the second line parallel with the first line, and mark for a square cutoff.

Cut the first shelf, and sand the edges smooth. Use the first shelf as a template and draw the next two shelves. Use the framing square to draw a line dividing one of the shelves in half, and cut.

2. Drill the holes.

On one of the shelves, mark for centers of holes 3 inches in from each corner. Mark for another hole in the center of the shelf's width and 33 inches from one end. Drill with a 2-inch hole saw, then use the shelf as a template to mark for holes in the other shelves.

3. Apply edging.
Cover the plywood edges with veneer tape. Attach it by applying glue to the plywood edge and holding the veneer tape in place with masking tape (see page 50).

4. Cut the conduit standards.
Cut five pieces of 2-inch conduit (the nonthreaded kind) to 54 inches or so, depending on how tall you want the unit to be. Use a hacksaw or a tubing cutter. To prepare the pipe for painting, first sand the conduit with a loose sheet of medium-grit sandpaper.

5. Sand and paint standards and shelves.
Sand the shelves smooth. Apply a coat of primer and two coats of enamel paint to conduit, couplings, and shelves. If you like the silvery look of galvanized conduit and couplings, just leave them alone; the finish will last.

6. Slip on shelves, attach couplings.
At the bottom of each standard, slip on a coupling and tighten the setscrews. Slip the bottom shelf onto all five standards, and slide it down. Slip on couplings for the next shelf, and measure to see that they are all at the same height. Slip on the shelf. Repeat for all the shelves. If the standards fit tightly into the holes, the unit will be stable. If it wobbles, anchor it to a wall with angle brackets and screws.

BUILDING AN ENTERTAINMENT CENTER

This handsome unit hides a TV and a stereo behind cabinet doors, and it includes plenty of shelves for storage and display.

The central cabinet has adjustable shelves 2 feet wide—large enough for standard stereo components and a medium-sized TV. The shallow shelves leave a 3-inch gap at the rear for wires and ventilation. These doors are slabs trimmed with half-round molding, but you could make panel doors instead (see pages 42–43).

YOU'LL NEED
TIME: Two days.
SKILLS: Making doors, measuring and cutting, cutting dadoes.
TOOLS: Power saw, drill, hammer, framing square.

1. Make the side panels.
Cut two pieces of ³/₄-inch plywood to 22×80 inches. Cut a ³/₈ × ³/₄-inch rabbet along the top and side of each (make them mirror images of each other), as well as two ³/₈ × ³/₄-inch dadoes (see pages 38–41). Attach metal shelving standards (see page 62).

2. Assemble the shelf system.
Cut plywood shelves 18 inches deep and 24 inches wide, and apply screen molding to the front edges (see page 50). Working on a flat surface, attach the fixed shelves with glue and 6d finish nails. Cut ¼-inch plywood for the back; attach it with 3d finish nails.

3. Add the stiles and rails.
Cut two 1×2 stiles, and attach them with glue and 6d finish nails, allowing the outside edges to overhang the plywood by ¹/₈ inch. Cut rails—1×6 for the bottom, 1×2 for the middle, and 1×4 for the top—to fit between the stiles, and attach them the same way.

4. Make the doors.

To make trimmed slab doors, start with warp-free plywood. Cut them to size so that there will be a consistent reveal of the stiles and rails when the doors are installed. (Take into account the molding you will use for the bottom and top.) Apply veneer tape to the edges (see page 50). Trim the door by attaching miter-cut pieces of molding with glue and small brads.

5. Make the open shelf units.

Cut four plywood vertical pieces to the same height as the side panels (Step 1) but only 12 inches deep. Cut rabbets and dadoes and install the metal shelf standards as as in Step 1. Assemble shelves and the back pieces as in Step 2. Add stiles and rails as in Step 3, except install the stiles flush against the edges of the middle unit, as shown.

6. Add the top molding.

Attach the open shelf units to the middle unit with 1¼-inch screws, and attach the entire unit to the wall by driving screws through the back panel and into studs. Trim out the top with cove molding. Rip angled bracing from a 2×2 to back the molding. Make miter cuts for the outside corners (see inset) and coped joints for the inside corners (see page 30).

7. Install the base molding and finish.

To make the unit appear built-in, purchase molding that matches the base molding in the room. Install it the way you did the top molding (Step 6).

Give all the parts a coat of primer and two coats of enamel paint, or apply stain and then a polyurethane finish if you used hardwood plywood. Then hang the doors (see page 44-47).

ADDING A RADIATOR COVER

An old steam or hot-water radiator can be an eyesore that takes up valuable space. This cover transforms a radiator into an attractive shelf and makes it more efficient because of the heat-reflecting metal surfaces above and behind the radiator. With it, less heat is lost through the rear wall. The spaces above and below the front grid cause warm air to move away from the radiator via convection: Cold air enters from below, and warm air is pushed out the top.

YOU'LL NEED

TIME: Most of a day.
SKILLS: Measuring and cutting, connecting with screws.
TOOLS: Power saw, drill, hammer, utility knife, square, level, staple gun, tin snips.

1. Measure the area.
The radiator cover should be at least 2 inches above the top of the radiator and at least 1 inch from the sides and front. If you turn the radiator handle often, leave an access space so you won't have to remove the whole cover to reach the handle.

2. Assemble the frame.
For each side, cut two upright 1×2s. Cut two horizontal 1×2 rails, 3 inches shorter than the frame will be. For each end (you may need only one end if the radiator side is against a wall) cut two horizontals 3¾ inches shorter than the frame width.

Assemble the frames, providing a 3-inch space at the floor and a 2-inch space at the top. Drill pilot holes and drive 3-inch trimhead screws, or fasten with dowels (see pages 36–37). If the cover is longer than 3 feet, install an intermediate upright so the metal grid doesn't sag. Paint the frames.

3. Attach cleats.

To add strength to the top, install cleats on the wall for the top to rest on. Position the frames where they will go, and use a level to mark lines between them. Attach a 1×2 cleat by drilling pilot holes and driving 2-inch screws into the studs.

4. Attach metal grid.

Purchase sheets of perforated sheet metal; "union jack" is a popular pattern. Cut the sheets 1/2 inch longer than the openings. Attach them to the back of the frames with 9/16-inch staples every inch or so. You may have to finish driving them with a hammer.

5. Install insulating-foil backing.

Purchase insulating foil, which comes in rolls. Cut it with a utility knife, and staple it to the wall(s) behind the radiator with a staple gun. If you have plaster walls, you may need to fasten the foil to 1×2 cleats screwed into wall studs.

6. Attach under-shelf metal.

Cut the top out of 3/4-inch plywood; it should overhang the frame an inch or so. Cut a piece of sheet metal 1 inch smaller than the top and attach it to the underside of the top with staples.

7. Assemble the parts.

Join the front frame piece to the end piece(s) by drilling pilot holes and driving 1 1/4-inch trimhead screws. Place the frame pieces next to the radiator. Attach the top to the frame with 1 1/4-inch trimhead screws, then attach it to the cleats in the same way. Cover the plywood edges of the top with 3/4-inch screen molding (see page 50). Give the unit a final coat of paint, being careful not to paint the reflective metal.

INSTALLING CLOSET ORGANIZERS

A standard closet, with a single rod and shelf, wastes valuable space. Improve your usable storage by dividing it into sections tailored to suit your needs.

Divide hanging clothes into two or three groups according to height. Determine how much width each group requires; make sure the clothes will not be crammed together. Figure how much shelf space you need for sweaters, as well as rack space for shoes. You may want to purchase plastic storage boxes that fit on the shelves. Allow extra room throughout for future purchases.

Draw a diagram of your shelf system on graph paper, and make a materials list that includes ³/₄-inch plywood and edging for the shelves and upright supports (see the box on page 99 for typical shelf measurements). Use 1×2 for cleats and heel stops, 1¹/₄-inch dowels for hanging rods, metal standards and clips for the shelves, and hardware to hold rods.

Cut the uprights for the tower of shelves, and install metal standards for adjustable shelves (see page 62). Fasten the fixed shelves with glue and 8d finish nails. Position the shelf unit, check for square, and attach it to the wall with angle brackets and screws.

Cut the top shelf to fit between the side walls and the middle shelf to fit to the shelf tower. Attach 1×2 cleats to the wall, and attach the shelves to the cleats. Cut and install closet rods using special closet-rod hardware. Cut and attach shoe shelves at about a 30-degree angle, and nail 1×2s for heel stops.

YOU'LL NEED

TIME: A full day.
SKILLS: Measuring and cutting, leveling, attaching with nails.
TOOLS: Power saw, level, drill, hacksaw, hammer, square.

cleat

1¹/₄" closet rod

top shelf

1¹/₄" closet rod

76–82"

miscellaneous storage

adjustable shelf standards

middle shelf

³/₄" plywood

1¹/₄" closet rod

rod/shelf bracket

38–40"

shoe shelf

heel stop

space for suits, coats, and dresses

fixed shelf

space for shirts and blouses

space for pants and skirts

pull-out basket

space for pants and skirts

shoe rack

Wire closet organizers are easy to install, need no painting, and may actually be cheaper than the materials needed to build wood shelves. You may be able to buy a kit that fits your space with little cutting.

Take a drawing with exact dimensions to a home center and ask a salesperson to supply you with all the parts. You'll need shelves with hanger rods, wall-hanging clips, end clips, diagonal supports for shelves over 2 feet, and rubber caps to cover any exposed metal rod ends. You may also want a drawer unit.

Install the drawer tower first; then cut shelves to fit above and on both sides of it. Draw level lines on the walls, install the clips so they are level, and then snap the shelves into the clips.

Install wall-hanging clips at the rear wall. Some types have plastic anchors so you can screw them directly into drywall. Mount hardware to wall studs when possible. Install end wall clips at the side walls.

Cut the shelves with a hacksaw or a pair of bolt cutters. After snapping the shelves in place, install shelf supports.

MEASUREMENTS

COMMON CLOSET SIZES

A closet for hanging clothes is usually 24 inches deep. Make shelves 18 inches deep. Shirts, blouses, and skirts usually require 36 vertical inches. For men's and women's suits and slacks, allow 42 inches. Coats and dresses are usually 54 inches long. Robes and long dresses may require up to 68 inches.

MAKING A DESK AND ORGANIZER

A flush door (one that is smooth, without any panels) makes a serviceable desk surface when placed on two drawer filing cabinets. If it is made of oak or birch, you can stain it and apply a coat of polyurethane. The handy shelf system above it requires careful planning and plenty of dado cuts.

YOU'LL NEED

TIME: A day to make both pieces.
SKILLS: Measuring and cutting, cutting dadoes, gluing and trimming plastic laminate.
TOOLS: Power saw, square, paintbrush, laminate trimmer or router, sanding block.

laminate roller

laminate

contact cement

router

masking tape

miter cut

1. Glue laminate onto the door.
Cut a piece of plastic laminate about an inch wider and longer than the door. To prevent cracks, score the cut line with a knife before cutting. Use a paintbrush to spread an even coat of contact cement to the back of the laminate and the face of the door. Allow it to dry. With a helper, carefully place the laminate on the door so that all of the door is covered; once placed, you cannot budge it. Use a laminate roller or rolling pin to ensure bonding.

2. Trim and edge the door.
Trim overhanging laminate so its edge is flush with the door edge, with a laminate trimmer or a router equipped with a laminate-trimming bit (see inset). Clean up rough edges with a sanding block.

Use 1×2 hardwood to edge the door. Make miter cuts at the corners, and attach the edging by applying wood glue and taping it in place until the glue dries (see page 50).

3

3. Plan the shelf system.

On a sheet of graph paper, draw a complete plan of the shelf system. The plan shown *above* has several compartments for full sheets of paper, as well as compartments for CDs and computer disks. Make the spaces an inch or so wider than the items to be stored.

Make the shelf unit at least 11 inches deep to accommodate full sheets of paper. To figure the exact sizes of each piece, take into account the thickness of the plywood—½ inch—as well as the ⅛-inch-deep dadoes. Double-check your figures; it's easy to make a mistake.

4

4. Cut and assemble the shelves.

Cut the top and bottom pieces, and cut ⅛ × ½-inch dadoes and rabbets to accept the uprights (see pages 38–41). Cut the vertical shelf standards to length, and cut dadoes to support the shelves. Saw the larger shelves, cutting dadoes where necessary.

Temporarily assemble the pieces by pushing them into place, and double-check measurements for the smaller pieces. Attach all the pieces with wood glue and 3d finish nails. Cut a ¼-inch plywood back, and attach it with glue and 3d finish nails. Paint the interior to match the desktop laminate.

5

5. Apply edging.

Cut pieces of ½-inch molding to cover the plywood edges. Install the two long horizontal pieces first, then all the vertical pieces, then all the horizontals. Use fast-setting wood glue to avoid nailing: Press the edging into place, remove and allow to dry slightly, then reapply.

ADDING A WINDOW SEAT

With open shelves on both sides, this seat makes a flat window feel like a bay window. A seat 20 inches deep affords ample room for lounging. Two large drawers underneath are handy for storing linens, and the shelves hold a small collection of books, making this a cozy reading nook.

Begin by removing base molding from the wall; cut and reinstall it on the uncovered wall sections after installing the unit. Mark studs so you can install brackets for holding the shelves and seat in place (see page 74).

YOU'LL NEED

TIME: A day to build and paint.
SKILLS: Cutting dadoes and rabbets, squaring, attaching with nails and screws.
TOOLS: Power saw, saber saw, drill, hammer, square, level.

1. Build the box and face frame.

From ¾-inch plywood, cut two side pieces, a top piece, and a back piece to the dimensions shown. Working on a flat surface, fasten the back to the side pieces by driving 2-inch screws through the back and into the sides. Set the top piece in place and drive 2-inch screws through it and into the sides and back.

Cut 1×4 and 1×2 rails and stiles to the dimensions *shown*. Position the bottom rail so it runs past the box sides ¼ inch on each side, and so the center piece is in its exact middle. Attach by drilling pilot holes, applying wood glue, and driving 6d finish nails. Attach the stiles and the top rail in the same way; the top rail will be 1½ inches above the plywood pieces. Cut a top piece to fit, and attach it with wood glue and 6d finish nails. Cut four strips for the glide bases, and attach them with 1¼-inch screws.

2
¾" plywood top 11⅛" wide

ledger

adjustable standards

1×6

1×2

¾" ×9½" plywood

ledger

1×4

1×4 kick plate

¾" plywood, 11⅛" wide, double with 1×2s sandwiched between

2. Build the shelves.

Decide on the height and width of the shelf units; in a narrow room with a low ceiling, you can run them to the side walls and from floor to ceiling. Make each shelf standard of two pieces of ¾-inch plywood, 11⅛ inches wide, with two 1×2s sandwiched in between (see pages 66–67). If you choose to support the shelves with dowels or pins, bore holes now (see page 67). (Metal standards can be installed later.) Build each shelf unit by first attaching one standard to the window seat using 3½-inch screws. Plumb it and attach it to the rear wall using angle brackets, then install the second standard. Install the kick plate and bottom shelf. Prefab the face frame, joining the pieces with glue and dowels (see page 67). Install the face frame by drilling pilot holes and driving 1⅝-inch trimhead screws every 6 inches. Build the shelves using 9½-inch plywood with 1×2 edging.

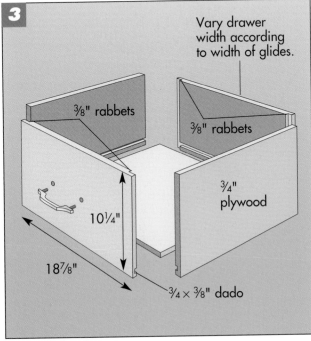

3
Vary drawer width according to width of glides.

⅜" rabbets

⅜" rabbets

¾" plywood

10¼"

18⅞"

¾ × ⅜" dado

4

3. Build the drawers.

Measure the openings in the base unit, and build drawers to fit (see pages 48–49). Use ¾-inch plywood for all the pieces. Check the drawer glides to see how much smaller than the opening the drawers should be. Install the drawer pull.

4. Install the drawers.

Attach drawer glides to the drawers and to the drawer unit (see page 49), and slide in the drawers.

Give the entire unit two coats of enamel paint, or stain it and apply a polyurethane finish. Have a cushion (or cushions) made by an upholsterer.

ADDING WRAPAROUND SHELVES

In rooms where every square inch counts, shelves set well above the floor make more sense. Combine them with overhead shelves set around the perimeter of the room, and you can equip a small space with a surprising amount of shelf area. You don't even need generous ceiling height: The most compact ranch home has enough room for one shelf set above the door and window casing.

YOU'LL NEED

TIME: A day to install and trim six or seven shelves.
SKILLS: Measuring and cutting, biscuit-joining, leveling, finding studs, attaching with screws.
TOOLS: Power saw, level, drill, stud finder.

Customize ready-made shelves.
Buy ready-made MDF shelving (see pages 14–15), ³/₄-inch thick and 10 inches deep. Finish with gloss or semigloss enamel for crisp good looks and easy cleaning. Then give it a finished look by trimming the edges with a stained hardwood molding. Choose shelf brackets to suit your style.

1. Attach the brackets.
Use a level to make horizontal pencil lines indicating the top of each shelf. (So the lines will not be visible.) Use a stud finder to locate studs, and mark for them. Install each bracket ³/₄ inch below the line, driving screws at least 1½ inches into studs. At the corner, install a triangular shim.

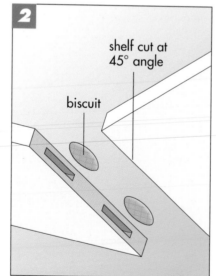

2. Install the shelves.
Cut the shelves to fit, and set them on top of the brackets. If your wall is noticeably wavy, scribe a line at the back of the shelf, and cut with a saber saw so it will fit tightly against the wall. Paint the shelves. At corners, cut both pieces at 45-degree angles and join them with biscuits (see page 37).

3. Add the trim.
Stain and apply polyurethane finish to the hardwood molding. Cut the molding with a miter saw (see page 30), making 45-degree miters at the corners. Install the molding by drilling pilot holes and driving 3d finish nails. Countersink the nails, and fill the holes with color-matched putty.

MAKING STACKABLE SHELVES

These modules are easily moved and restacked. If you need to, you always can build more. Make modules of at least two heights—10 and 14 inches high are common dimensions—to accommodate your books. For yearbooks, magazines, and photo albums, you may need a module that is even taller. You will need one top piece for each tower of stackable shelves. Choose your lumber carefully: Twisted boards will not line up well. Use a hardwood such as oak and stain it, or build out of pine and give it at least two coats of enamel paint.

YOU'LL NEED

TIME: Three hours per module.
SKILLS: Measuring and marking, squaring, drilling straight holes, cutting dadoes and rabbets.
TOOLS: Power saw, square, drill, drill jig, hammer.

Versatile storage.
If you build carefully, these units will fit together quite snugly. However, if you stack more than three, they may become unstable. If that happens, use angle brackets and screws to attach the top shelf to the wall.

Building with dowels and dadoes.

Use 1×12 for the sides, shelves, and top. Cut the side pieces to the height of the module (the usable shelf space will be 1¾ inches shorter), and the shelf to the width, minus ¾ inch. Cut a ⅜ × ⅜-inch rabbet along the inside back edges of the side pieces and the upper back edge of the shelf. Cut a ¾ × ⅜-inch dado in each side piece, located 1 inch up from the bottom (see pages 38–41).

Attach the shelf in the dadoes, using wood glue and 4d finish nails, checking for square. Cut a back out of ¼-inch plywood to fit into the rabbets, and attach it with wood glue and 3d finish nails.

Use a drill and jig (see page 36) to drill holes as *shown*. Also drill holes under the top piece, being careful not to drill too deeply. Insert dowels (but don't glue them) as you stack the modules.

top for uppermost module only

⅜" × ⅜" rabbet

¼" plywood, 30×12¼"

⅜" × ⅜" rabbet

1×12

14"

1×12

1×12

¾" × ⅜" dado

dry-fit dowels

30"

BUILDING A BASEMENT WINE RACK

Most basements are cool and dark—ideal for storing wine. Here's a rack that stores your favorite vintages the right way: bottles on their sides.

Use the dark brown heartwood of redwood or cedar so it will not rot in damp conditions. Apply a sealer-preservative, paying special attention to the feet.

Although this unit has feet for stability, it is a good idea to anchor it to the wall or to joists.

YOU'LL NEED

TIME: Two or three days.
SKILLS: Measuring and cutting, cutting curves, cutting dadoes, attaching with screws.
TOOLS: Power saw, drill, hole saw, square, level.

1. Cut the front stringers.

Each 1×6 will produce two front stringers. Along the length of a 1×6, draw a line down the exact center. Mark the centerline 4 inches from one end, then every 3½ inches. The last line should be 4 inches from the other end. Use a hole saw to cut a 1½-inch hole in the center of each mark. Rip-cut the boards in half, along the centerline. Repeat these steps to make the other stringers.

2. Mark for the rear stringers.

Cut pieces of 1×3 to the same length as the front stringers. On one of the boards, draw a line ¾ inch from the edge all along its length. Mark the center-lines as you did in Step 1, first at 4 inches and then every 3½ inches. Cut a 4-inch circle from a piece of cardboard to use as a template, and use it to mark for scallops as *shown*, with the bottom of the arcs at the intersections of the line and the marks.

3. Cut the rear stringers.

Use a saber saw or jigsaw to cut the scallops (see pages 25, 27). Work carefully and methodically, to cut smooth curves. Make sure the blade is at an exact 90-degree angle to the saw base. Use the first piece as a template to mark for the other rear stringers, and cut them the same way. Sand the cutouts smooth.

4. Notch and cut the standards.

Clamp two 2×8s together, and mark them for notches. Start the lowest notch 4⅜ inches from the bottom, and space the others every 6½ inches. Cut ¾-inch-deep notches on one edge of both boards, then flip the boards over and cut notches at the same locations on the other side.

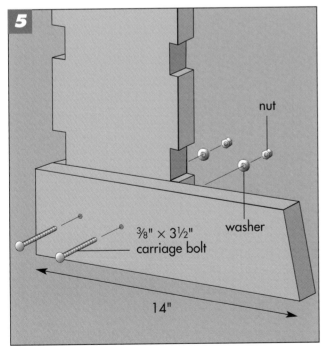

5. Attach the feet.

Cut pieces of 2×8 to the dimensions shown. Clamp a foot onto the bottom of one standard, with the bottom edges flush; drill holes, and attach with two ⅜ × 3½-inch carriage bolts. Repeat for the other foot.

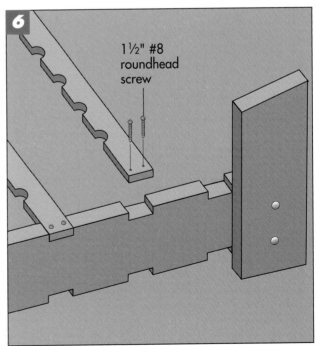

6. Attach the stringers.

Lay the standards on edge, and set the front stringers in the notches. At each joint, drill two pilot holes and drive two 1½-inch #8 roundhead brass screws. Repeat for the rear stringers.

GLOSSARY

For words not listed here, or for more about those that are, refer to the index, pages 110–112.

Actual dimension. The true size of a piece of lumber, after milling and drying. *See Nominal dimension.*

Bevel cut. An angle cut through the thickness of a piece of wood.

Biscuit joiner. A power tool used to cut incisions in lumber into which flat, football-shaped wooden biscuits are glued.

Blind dado. A channel cut across the grain that stops short of one or both edges of the workpiece.

Building codes. Community ordinances governing the manner in which a home may be constructed or modified. Most codes are primarily concerned with fire and health, with separate sections relating to electrical, plumbing, and structural work.

Butt joint. The joint formed by two pieces of material when fastened end-to-end, end-to-face, or end-to-edge.

Carcass. The box-like outer body or framework of a cabinet or shelf.

Casing. Trimming around a door, window, or other opening.

Cleat. A length of board attached to strengthen or add support to a structure.

Counterbore. To drive a screw below the surface of the surrounding wood. The void created is filled later with putty or is plugged.

Countersink. To drive the head of a nail or screw so that the top is flush with the surface of the surrounding wood.

Cove. A concave form, as in the face of a style of molding.

Crosscut. To saw a piece of lumber perpendicular to its length and/or its grain.

Dado joint. A joint formed when the end of one member fits into a groove cut partway through the face of another.

Dowel. A piece of small-diameter wood rod, used to reinforce joints.

Doweling jig. A metal device that clamps onto a workpiece edge or end and aids in accurately locating and drilling holes for dowels.

Drywall. A basic interior building material consisting of sheets of pressed gypsum faced with heavy paper on both sides. Also known as wallboard, gypsum board, plasterboard, and Sheetrock®.

Edging. Strips of wood or veneer used to cover the edges of plywood or boards.

End grain. The ends of wood fibers that are exposed at the ends of boards.

Face frame. The front structure of a cabinet or chest of drawers made of stiles and rails; it surrounds the door panels or drawers.

Filler. A paste-like compound used to hide surface imperfections in wood. Another type—pore filler—levels the surface of wood that has a coarse grain.

Flush. On the same plane as, or level with, a surrounding surface.

Grit. The abrasive material bonded to a piece of sandpaper. Grits are designated by numbers, such as 120-grit and 240-grit. The a higher the number the finer the abrasive.

Hardwood. Lumber that comes from leaved, deciduous trees, such as oak and maple.

Joist. Horizontal framing members that support a floor and/or ceiling.

Kerf. The void created by the blade of a saw as it cuts partially through a piece of material.

Laminate. A hard plastic decorative veneer applied to cabinets and shelves. Can refer to a material formed by building up layers, as in plywood—or to the process of applying a veneer to a surface, such as a countertop.

Lap joint. The joint formed when one member overlaps another.

Layout. A plan, often sketched on the wall or floor, showing where cabinets or shelves will be located.

Ledger. A horizontal strip (usually lumber) that's used to provide support for the ends or edges of other members.

Level. The condition that exists when any type of surface is at true horizontal. Also a tool used to determine level.

Linear foot. The simple length of a board or piece of molding (in contrast to board foot, which refers to volume).

Load-bearing wall. A wall that supports a wall or roof section on the floor above. Do not cut or remove a stud in a load-bearing wall without proper alternative support. *See also Partition Wall.*

MDF (Medium Density Fiberboard). Made of very fine wood chips, this material is available in 12- and 16-inch-wide pieces often used for shelving.

Miter joint. The joint formed when two members meet that have been cut at the same angle.

Molding. A strip of wood, usually small-dimensioned, used to cover exposed edges or as decoration.

Mortise. A shallow cutout in a board usually used to recess hardware, such as hinges.

Nominal dimension. The stated size of a piece of lumber, such as a 2×4 or a 1×12. The actual dimension is somewhat smaller.

On-center (OC). The distance from the center of one regularly spaced framing member or hole to the center of the next.

1-by (2-by). Refers to nominal one- or two-inch thick lumber of any width, length, or type of wood. Actual thickness are ¾ inch and 1½ inch, respectively.

Particleboard. Panels made from compressed wood chips and glue.

Partition wall. Unlike a load-bearing wall, a partition supports no structure above it and can therefore be removed.

Pilot hole. A small hole drilled into a wooden member to avoid splitting the wood when driving a screw or nail.

Plumb. The condition that exists when a member is truly vertical.

Rabbet. A step-shaped cut made along the edge of a piece of wood, used to join boards tightly.

Rails. Horizontal pieces of a cabinet facing.

Rip. To saw lumber or sheet goods parallel to the grain pattern.

Roughing-in. The framing stage of a carpentry project. This framework later is concealed in the finishing stages.

Rout. To shape edges or cut grooves, using a router.

Scribe. To use a geometry compass or scrap of wood to transfer the shape or dimension of an object to a piece of wood to be cut.

Scratch sealer. A protective, usually clear, coating applied to wood or metal.

Setting nails. Driving the heads of nails slightly below the surface of the wood.

Shim. A thin strip or wedge of wood or other material used to fill a gap between two adjoining components or to help establish level or plumb.

Sliding door track. A set of grooves or runners along the front of a cabinet at top and bottom that hold sliding cabinet doors in place and permit them to slide.

Spacer. A piece of finished wood or particleboard used to fill in the space at the end of a run of cabinets.

Square. The condition that exists when one surface is at a 90-degree angle to another. Also, a tool used to determine square.

Stiles. Vertical members of a door assembly or cabinet facing.

Stringer. The main structural member of a stairway.

Stud finder. Electronic or magnetic tool that locates studs within a finished wall.

Studs. Vertical 2×4 or 2×6 framing members spaced at regular intervals within a wall.

Template. A pattern to follow when re-creating a precise shape.

Toe kick. Indentation at the bottom of a floor-based cabinet. Also known as toe space.

Toe-nail. To drive a nail at an angle, so as to hold together two pieces of material.

Veneer. A thin layer of decorative wood laminated to the surface of a more common wood.

Veneer tape. A ribbon of reinforced wood veneer applied to plywood or other rough wood with glue or heat-sensitive adhesive.

Wall anchor. A fastener such as the toggle bolt or Molly that is used to secure objects to hollow walls, or a concrete anchor used to secure objects to concrete or masonry walls.

Warp. Any of several lumber defects caused by uneven shrinkage of wood cells.

INDEX

METRIC CONVERSIONS

U.S. UNITS TO METRIC EQUIVALENTS			METRIC UNITS TO U.S. EQUIVALENTS		
To Convert From	Multiply By	To Get	To Convert From	Multiply By	To Get
Inches	25.4	Millimeters	Millimeters	0.0394	Inches
Inches	2.54	Centimeters	Centimeters	0.3937	Inches
Feet	30.48	Centimeters	Centimeters	0.0328	Feet
Feet	0.3048	Meters	Meters	3.2808	Feet
Yards	0.9144	Meters	Meters	1.0936	Yards
Miles	1.6093	Kilometers	Kilometers	0.6214	Miles
Square inches	6.4516	Square centimeters	Square centimeters	0.1550	Square inches
Square feet	0.0929	Square meters	Square meters	10.764	Square feet
Square yards	0.8361	Square meters	Square meters	1.1960	Square yards
Acres	0.4047	Hectares	Hectares	2.4711	Acres
Square miles	2.5899	Square kilometers	Square kilometers	0.3861	Square miles
Cubic inches	16.387	Cubic centimeters	Cubic centimeters	0.0610	Cubic inches
Cubic feet	0.0283	Cubic meters	Cubic meters	35.315	Cubic feet
Cubic feet	28.316	Liters	Liters	0.0353	Cubic feet
Cubic yards	0.7646	Cubic meters	Cubic meters	1.3079	Cubic yards
Cubic yards	764.55	Liters	Liters	0.0013	Cubic yards
Fluid ounces	29.574	Milliliters	Milliliters	0.0338	Fluid ounces
Quarts	0.9464	Liters	Liters	1.0567	Quarts
Gallons	3.7854	Liters	Liters	0.2642	Gallons
Drams	1.7718	Grams	Grams	0.5644	Drams
Ounces	28.350	Grams	Grams	0.0353	Ounces
Pounds	0.4536	Kilograms	Kilograms	2.2046	Pounds

To convert from degrees Fahrenheit (F) to degrees Celsius (C), first subtract 32, then multiply by ⁵⁄₉.

To convert from degrees Celsius to degrees Fahrenheit, multiply by ⁹⁄₅, then add 32.